RAMBLES IN

Rambles
in the West of Ireland

by

WILLIAM BULFIN

THE MERCIER PRESS
DUBLIN and CORK

The Mercier Press Limited
4 Bridge Street, Cork
25 Lower Abbey Street, Dublin 1

First published 1907
This selection © The Mercier Press 1979.

ISBN 0 85342 585 X

Printed in the Republic of Ireland by The Kerryman Ltd., Tralee

CONTENTS

1

Around Lough Gill — Knocknarea — Sligo — The Lake —
The Hills — The Valley of O'Rourke — Dromahair —
O'Rourke's Table.

I had decided on a tour into northern Connacht, so with
a mixture of 'the white wind from the South and the brown
wind from the West' on my shoulder, I pulled out on one of
the main roads leading through Ely O'Carroll and faced for
the Shannon. Lough Gill was my destination, and I shaped
my course as follows: Athlone, Roscommon, Sligo, Dromahair.

Had I hearkened to the oracular guidance of a road
book, edited by a West Briton, which had cost me a shilling,
I would have gone to Sligo by train, for, according to the
book, the road from Dublin to Sligo is 'an uninteresting
route and road indifferent'. But a month's experience had
taught me that the most I could expect from this book was
an occasional piece of unconscious humour.

The 'uninteresting route' alluded to above is really one
of the most interesting in all Ireland. It crosses the magnificent plain of Meath, passing close to Tara. It takes you
past scores of historic and beautiful places in fair Westmeath of the lakes. It leads you over the most picturesque
of the Longford uplands; and whether you decide to cross
the Shannon at Lanesborough or at Carrick, it shows
you the hills of Annaly of the O'Ferralls, and gives you the
choice of a look at beautiful Lough Ree, or a ramble
through the delightful country between Newton Forbes
and Drumsna.

When you cross the Shannon the Sligo road takes you over the Connacht plains and brings you within sight of royal Cruachain. It leads you into Boyle, and thence through the Pass of the Curlews, or you have an alternative road to Sligo round the northern spur of the Curlews by the rock of Doon, and the shore of Lough Key and to Sligo by Knocknarea.

'An uninteresting route?' Not if you are Irish and know some of the history of your land, and feel some pleasure in standing beside the graves of heroes and on ground made sacred by their heroism. Not if you delight to see hay-making, and the turf cutting, and in observing the simple, beautiful life of rural Ireland. Not if you feel at home among the boys and girls at the cross-roads in the evening time, or if you know how to enjoy a drink of milk and a chat with the old people across the half door, or on a stool beside the hearth. Not if you love the woods and the mantling glory of waving corn ripening in the sun, and the white winding roads made cool on the hottest day by the shade of flower-laden hedges.

But if you are one of those tired and tiresome souls desirous only of treading in the footsteps of the cheap trippers who follow one another like sheep, if you have no eye of your own for the beautiful, and if you think it your duty to go out of your way to put money into the pockets of vampire railways, then in the name of all the Philistines and seoinini take the train, or stay away out of the country altogether, or go to some peepshow and surfeit your narrow photographic soul on 'views'.

The road over the Curlew Mountains from Boyle is a grand one. If you are an average roadster you can pedal up the greater part of the gradient. They tell a story in Boyle of a man who negotiated the mountains in night time without becoming aware of it. He said, when asked how he had found the roads, that they were all right, but that he thought he had met a sort of a long hill somewhere. He was either a champion rider or a humorist.

Anyhow the ordinary tourist will have to get off his machine for a few steep zigzags. The rest is nothing more formidable than a good tough climb. You can rest now and then and admire the spreading plains behind you to the eastward. You can see into Mayo and Galway to your right, and Boyle is just below you, the old abbey lifting its twelfth century gables over the trees. To your left is beautiful Lough Key.

A little higher up you come to the verge of the battle-field of the Curlews. They call it Deerpark or some such history-concealing name now. Ballaghboy is what the annalists call it. You can see the stone erected on the spot where Clifford, the English general fell. You can see where the uncaged Eagle of the North prepared for his swoop, and the heart within you leaps as your eye follows adown the slope the line of his victorious onset. God's rest and peace be with your soul, Red Hugh! You were a sensible, practical patriot, although there is no big tower one hundred and goodness knows how many feet high erected to your memory on Ireland's ground. And although you had no blatant press to give you high-sounding names and sing your praises to the world, you believed that liberty was worth the best blood in your veins, and you did not waste breath on windy resolutions. And when you raised your hand, it was not the everlasting hat that you held out in it to the gaze of the nations, for it had that in it which was worthy of Ireland and you. 'Twas something that gleamed and reddened and blazed and that flashed the light of wisdom and duty into the souls of manly men.

After passing Ballaghboy the road leads upward into the fastnesses of the Curlews, where for a while the world is

9

shut off. The health-clad summits of the peaks hem you in. For about a mile you ride in this solitude and then suddenly there is a turn and the world comes back again. Below you the valleys and woods are alternating in the near distance. In front of you is a green hillside dotted with farm houses. There, too, is Lough Arrow, and beyond it, always in the hazy distance, is the purple bulk of Slieveanierin and the grey masses of Knocknarea and Benbulben. Ten minutes will bring you to the town of Ballinafad. The road from here to Sligo is a grand one for the cyclist. It is smooth and level nearly all the way.

After a few miles of this pleasant road you come to an ancient-looking demesne. The timber is old and lofty, the wall along the roadside is moss-grown, the undergrowth beneath the oaks and pines is thick and tangled. This is the Filliat or Folliard estate. It is where the scene of 'Willie Reilly' is laid. Here lived the 'great Squire Folliard' and his lovely daughter—the heroine of one of the most popular of Anglo-Irish love tales, and the subject of a ballad that has been sung in many lands:

Oh! rise up, Willie Reilly, and come along with me!

The suggestion of the metre must have come to the balladist in the lilt of some old traditional air of Connacht. I have nearly always heard it sung in the Irish traditional style—the style which lived on even after the Irish language had fallen into disuse. I have heard it sung in two hemispheres—by the winter firesides of Leinster and under the paraiso trees around the homes of the Pampas. I had followed it around the world, through the turf smoke and bone smoke—through the midges and mosquitoes and fire-flies. I was glad to find I had run it to earth at last, so to speak.

There is a gloom over the Folliat demesne now. The shadow of a great sorrow is on it. A few years ago a daughter

10

of the house went out on the lake in a boat to gather water lilies for her affianced lover, who was returning that evening to her after a long absence. She was drowned. They were to have been married in a day or two. The place has never been the same since then.

Collooney was meant by nature for great things. The river flowing by the town supplies it with immense water power. Under the rule of a free people, Collooney would be an important manufacturing centre. At present it is a mere village, struggling to keep the rooftrees standing. There are various mills beside the river, some of them I fear silenced forever. There is a woollen factory which is evidently trying conclusions with the shoddy from foreign mills. It is engaged in an uphill fight, but I hope it is winning. After passing the woollen factory, you cross the bridge, and, skirting a big hill, you drop down on the Sligo road, which takes you through one of the battlefields of '98.

The battle was fought close to the town. On 5 September 1798, the advance guard of Humbert's little army arrived at Collooney from Castlebar. Colonel Vereker, of the Limerick militia, was there from Sligo with some infantry, cavalry and artillery. He was beaten back to Sligo, and he lost his artillery. Humbert then marched to Dromahair and thence towards Manorhamilton, but suddenly wheeling he made for Longford to join the Granard men. Ballinamuck followed. Bartholomew Teeling and Matthew Tone (brother of Theobald Wolfe Tone) were among the Irish prisoners who surrendered with Humbert to Lord Cornwallis. They were executed a few days afterwards in Dublin.

Close beside the road on a rock hill they have erected a monument to Teeling. The statue, which is heroic in its expression, looks towards the 'Races of Castlebar' and reminds one of that splendid day. One uplifted hand grasps a battle-flag. The face is a poem, grandly eloquent in its

11

chiselling. You think you can catch the thought that was in the sculptor's mind. You can feel that his aim was to represent his hero looking out in fiery appeal and reproach over the sleeping West!

Sligo should by right be a great Irish seaport town, but if it had to live by its shipping interests it would starve in a week. Like Galway, it has had such a dose of British fostering and legislation that it seems to be afraid of ships, and the ships seem to be afraid of it. The city lives independently of its harbour, which it holds in reserve for brighter and greater days. There are, as far as one can judge, three Sligos— the Irish Sligo, the ascendancy Sligo and the Sligo which straddles between asendancy and nationalism. The Gaelic League is strong in the city, and one of the hardest workers in the West, when I was there, was Father Hynes.

Sligo is very picturesquely situated. Knocknarea guards it on one side and Benbulbin on the other. The hills which face the city to the northward are very beautiful, and beyond and above their fresh verdure are the rocky heights that beat off the keen and angry winds from the Atlantic. You ride down into the streets from a hill which overtops the steeples, and it is only when you come into the suburbs that you can see the bay. Clear and calm it looks from the Ballysadare road, but, alas! not a smoke cloud on the whole of it, not a sail in view, not a masthead over the roofs along the water front. The harbour is not, of course, entirely deserted. A steamer or a sailing ship comes in now and then. The same thing happens in Galway.

But I am not comparing the two cities, because there is no comparison between them. Galway drags on an existence. Sligo is very much alive. Galway went to the bad when its ocean trade was killed. Sligo is able to maintain itself by doing business with the district in which it is situated. Behind Galway there was no populous and fertile land near enough to be a support to business. Behind Sligo are the valleys which support a relatively thriving rural population.

You can spend a very pleasant day in and around Sligo, visiting places of historical interest or picturesque beauty. It was once a war-scourged district, and the scars are still there. The hills around have echoed to a hundred battle cries, some of which were raised for Ireland. At Ballysadare you will find waterfalls that are beautiful even to people who have seen photographs of Niagara and read of cascades in several fashionable countries. There is a ruined castle of the O'Connors, too, which has a history. It was shot to pieces in the days when Connacht was making its last fight for freedom, and it was never rebuilt. It was one of the outposts of Sligo and saw many a bloody fray in its time.

The sea runs in to Ballysadare and makes a bay around which you have to cycle to Knocknarea. Soon after coming to the slope of the hill you meet one of the queerest, wildest and most beautiful of glens. They call it after the mountain.

It is a wondrously romantic freak of nature, planted there in a cleft of the rock and walled off from the world, as if the Great Mother meant to lock it up and hide it away for her own use. It is thickly wooded, narrow and deep. The trees meet over the path in places, and the ferns touch you as you pass. The spirits of Knocknarea must love it. One can fancy how they made it their own centuries ago. A mystic poet might dream his life away in it, holding communion with the hero-dead of Connacht. It would also be a grand place for a botanist, or a 'man on his keeping' or an amateur distiller.

When you succeed in driving yourself out of the glen you ought to climb the mountain, on the top of which there is a cairn. There are people who will tell you that Queen Maeve was buried there and not at Cruachain. I

13

think they are in error. Perhaps it is one of the earlier kings of pagan Ireland that sleeps on Knocknarea.

Be that as it may, however, the cairn is a resting-place fit for a Monarch.. It looks down on wide Tir Fiachra where dwelt 'the music-loving hosts of fierce engagements'. Away to northward and eastward and southward are mountain and valley and river and lake and woodland. To the westward rolls the thundering ocean. The mountain has no partner in its glory. It stands proudly over the rocky coast in solitary grandeur. The mourners who erected the burial mound on its stately summit could not have chosen a more royal throne for their kingly dead. They could see the sungod smiling on it in the morning time before any other peak was crimsoned by his touch, and they caught the last flash of his golden spear upon it as he sank to sleep in the west. The fleecy shreds of vapour which float around it in the summer time adorn it like some silken scarf of gauze blown against the curls of a woman. The angry clouds of autumn and winter cap it. The lightning darts its fiery tongues upon it. The thunder bellows over it. And if the people of Tir Fiachra regarded all these things as being symbolic of the sunny or playful or tempestuous moods of their great one, it would only have been quite natural, for they were men and women of epic minds. Their lives were epic. Their fate was epic. Their history is epic.

And about Knocknarea itself there is an epic suggestiveness which you cannot miss if you climb the mountain. You cannot keep your hold upon the present while you are up there. You may smoke twentieth century tobacco and look down on twentieth century towns and railways and roads, but your thoughts are far away.

You can fancy the dead leader from the cairn on the summit gazing prophetically northward across Lough Gill and Breffni and Lough Erne into Ulster, or eastward towards

14

Cruachain and Tara. You wonder is the prophesying all over. Did it all end, was it all fulfilled, in the long ago? Or has a portion of it still to weave itself into form, now that so many bright gleams of the old temperament are kindling in the dreamers of our time?

A bearded stranger found me standing on a bridge in Sligo one morning and proposed to take me up Lough Gill in a boat. I asked him some questions in geography, and found his mind was virgin soil in this respect. All he could tell me was that the water underneath the bridge led to the lake, and that he was a boatman of vast experience and of the strictest honesty.

I asked him some questions in local history, and was informed that the history of Sligo is in books. So he had been told. None of the said history was in his possession, nor had he ever seen it, but he could positively assure me that his personal honesty was above suspicion, and that his boat was comfortable and safe, as the Mayor himself could testify. He offered to take me to Dromahair and back for six shillings. I said that I preferred to ride. This he solemnly told me was impossible. I knew better, for I had ridden it some weeks previously. But I did not tell this to the champion boatman of Sligo. I merely bade him good morning and said that I would mention him to my friends. He then offered to take me to Dromahair and back for five shillings. I shook my head. 'For four, then,' he called after me. I made no sign. 'For three,' he said, desperately. He drew a blank every time. Then he followed me and offered to tell me the best road. I knew it. Then in despair he turned away and left me to my fate.

I do not know if there are any other Lough Gill boatmen in Sligo. If there are, they do not seem to be overworked, for you seldom see a boat upon the lake. And yet it must be a delightful journey by water from the city to Dromahair.

15

The river which connects Lough Gill with the sea is short, but it is very beautiful. It flows between wooded hills and past smooth green lawns, and when it opens on the lake it is a new and abiding delight.

Opposite Dromahair, which is some distance away from the water, another river disembogues. You ascend this stream for about a mile until you meet a sort of jetty. Here you disembark, for you are within a few minutes walk of the Abbey Hotel. Such is one way to Dromahair. The way of the cyclist is either along the northern or southern shore around the lake. If you start by the northerly road you return to Sligo by the route which touches the southern shore of the lake. If you start by the southern road you return by the northern. A day will take you round Lough Gill comfortably. It is a run of about twenty miles—Irish miles, of course.

As you leave Sligo behind you and strike southward in the direction of Boyle the country looks bleak. It looks bleaker still as you wheel to the left at a cross-roads outside the city. The land is poor and the bare rock asserts itself over the clinging heather on the hills near the road. But have a little patience. Presently you come to a turn and creep down a steep incline, and then Lough Gill in all its loveliness and freshness and grandeur bursts upon your view. The change is so rapid and complete that for the first few moments you are bewildered.

But for goodness sake let us not hasten to compare it with anything or any place else. Let us take it on its own merits. The practice of comparing one beauty spot on this earth with another is hackneyed and, in the abstract, somewhat sickening. 'The Switzerland of Ireland' is a cry to be abhorred. So is 'How like Geneva!' So is 'How suggestive of the English lake country!' And another parrot cry is 'Oh! dear! How like the Rivera!' You cheapen Irish scenery

16

when you rush into such comparisons. There is none of it that you can flatter by calling it German or Italian or French or English names. This land of ours revels in beauty. She is a favoured child of nature; and I pity anyone born of her who would not prefer her loveliness to that of any other land, for it is second to none.

The change of scenery from the rather wild and barren country through which you passed after leaving the Boyle road opens full upon your view just when you have descended into the lake valley sufficiently to bring you on the level with the tops of the trees that cover the hills around the shore. Above the trees grow the heather and fern, and the weather-stained rocks crown the summits. Below you is the western end of the lake studded with islands, and each island is like a big hillock of verdure, so thickly do the trees grow together. In the autumn, when the different tints come on the foliage, each islet looks like a big nosegay set in the water, and the heather above the timber belt on the hills is covered with purple bloom.

The surface of the lake is smooth enough to reflect everything—the blue sky and the fleecy clouds and the verdant glory of the trees and ferns and meadows and the royal trappings of the heath, and the browns and greys of the beetling crags. All these tints mingle in the depths, gilded by the glad sunshine that fondly caresses them all. A rivulet murmurs and laughs softly to you as it tumbles down from the rocks under the cool shade of the briars and ferns. There are bird songs in the trees, and a rabbit scuttles swiftly across the road, and you hear the tap, tap of the thrush coming from the forest gloom beyond as he cracks a snail upon a stone and prepares his breakfast. You are alone with nature, and you enjoy it. But do not stop just yet.

Ride down the road to the water and look for a few moments up at the hills and along the lake between the islands. Then follow the road again upward through the woods until you come to a place where a broad pathway leads into the brush under the hazels. Leave your bicycle here—no one will meddle with it, even if they pass the way—and take the path which winds steeply up between the tree trunks at right angles to the road. The hart tongues, and the tall fronds of the wood ferns, and the wild violets and bluebells, brush your insteps; the hazel branches rustle against your head and shoulders, and the dried twigs snap under your feet.

Upward you bend your way across the little patches of light which the sun throws on the ground, as he peeps down through the branches of the oaks and pines, until you come to the level and wooded summit of the hills. You walk out on a rocky terrace and stand right over the lake, hundreds of feet over the pebbly strand which shines below you. This terrace gives you a splendid cross-view of Lough Gill.

The western and south-western creeks and bays are all in sight. You are far over the tree-tops of the islands. You can see the wide lawns of a park sloping downward to the river that flows on to Sligo and the farmsteads of the distant hills beyond which the Atlantic frets and swells. Here, indeed, you may rest and dream, or smoke and think of things. This is beauty undefiled, and you have it all to yourself. No tripper agency has yet discovered it; no railway company has yet fumigated it with coal smoke; no restaurant tout has yet daubed it with advertisements.

But you must not stay here for ever and ever, nor even for hours and hours. You have only just entered the charmed district of Lough Gill as yet, and there are many miles of it still to be seen. When you have had a good long draught of the loveliness which flows in upon you here, you tear yourself away as best you can from this terrace and go back to your bicycle.

The road now leaves the waterside and goes off round the mountain to Dromahair. When you leave the wood behind you the country falls into a jumble of hills and valleys and ravines and heathery mountain sides, and racing mountain streamlets which seam the rocks and start from under the ferns here and there, leaping wildly into the radiance of the day. I do not know how many years you could spend going over those roads without tiring of the beauty through which they take you. I have gone over them two or three times, and I want to go back there again.

The hills are of many colours, dark green and bright green with grass and scrub, brown and grey with rocks or purple with heather. Some of them are thickly wooded, others are bare and grim. You think you are going to get rid of them when you are climbing some steep reach of the smooth road; you fancy that when you have topped the incline in front of you there will be no more of them in your way.

But when you stand panting on the crest you will find another bewildering series of them still before you. Below you is a green valley, and above the fields laughs the gorse that crowns the slope. Beyond the yellow sheen of the blossoms is the dark shadow of another hillside and beyond that again the haze over another valley is purpled by the distance. And, over the valley the hilltops, one behind the other—all dim and far away—are peeping at you over each other's shoulders or frowning at you over each other's heads.

Bagairth a geinn thar dhruim a cheile.

That is exactly how the mountain must have looked to the poet—nodding their heads one from behind the other. They were piled up, just as they are around Lough Gill. They are grimly humorous in their persistency to hem a mortal in and plant themselves in his road, turn which way he would.

19

These are the Leitrim hills. They roll northward into Donega north-westward to Lough Erne and eastward to Cavan.

Long ago they were called Ui Briuin, Breifni or Breffr The territory was so called, says O'Mahony, from its beir possessed by the race of Ui Briuin. And the learned tran lator of Keating goes on to say: 'The Ui Briuin race derive their name from being descendants of Brian, King of Con nacht, in the fourth century'. Brian's posterity possesse the greater part of Connacht, and were called the Ui Briui race. Of this race were the O'Conors, the O'Rourkes, th O'Reillys, MacDermotts, etc., etc. And further he say 'The O'Rourkes and O'Reillys derived their descent fron Aedh Finn or Hugh the Fair, King of Connacht, who die A.D. 611. O'Rourke's country was called Breffni O'Rourk and O'Reilly's country was called Breffni O'Reilly.

There must have been a hardy race bred on those rugge hills. The mere work of marching over them would mak an athlete of a man or kill him. And when you come t push a bicycle around in Breffni you would want th muscle of four gallowglasses and the lungs of half a clan and the patience of Job. It is a magnificent country. It scenery is splendid in its many-sided variety, but it is not a easy to cycle through it as the Phoenix Park.

'Use makes master,' however, and you get used to Leitrin cycling difficulties. You accustom yourself to suddenly parting with your wheel and falling down a mountain with safety. You may fall gracefully and you may not, but the main point is to fall as safely as you can. If you can manage to fall into a wood, it is not bad; if into a growth of ferns, i is nicer, so long as you have a good distance to roll; it i grand to hear them rustling and breaking into sweet smelling shreds as you crash through them.

It is not unpleasant to slip off the road into a big bunchy tuft of heather, or into a moss-grown dyke. But it is

safe to go headlong into the Atlantic Ocean or dive into
mountain lake, or take a flight over a precipice into a
ap of rocks three or four hundred feet below. After being
me years in journalism a man's hide is fairly hard and
ick, but there are exigencies over which it will not rise
perior. It has its limits of endurance. I rode twice across
eitrim, and please God, some day or another I will ride
cross it again. It would be easier and safer work, of course,
your bicycle had a pair of wings, and if you had fourteen
r fifteen lives; but even with an ordinary wheel and one
fe it is grand.

It may be asked, why and how you fall down a moun-
ain? But no concise or definite reply can be given. Ask a
reat singer how or why he gets such glorious music out of
is throat, and what can he tell you, only that it comes? He
ay be able to give you a few superficial details, but no
vords of his can reach the kernel of the wonder. It is a gift.
And so with falling down mountains: it is a gift. Your
vheel slips or slides, or runs away, or you make too sharp a
urve, and all the rest is falling, falling, falling, and getting
o the bottom. While you are mending yourself and your
bicycle, you may wonder how you did it; but you can never
ell exactly. You can feel it and dream about it afterwards,
ut never realise it—until it happens again.

Dromahair was the capital of Breffni O'Rourke. The
O'Rourkes had castles at Leitrim, Carrickallen and Castle-
ar, but Dromahair was their chief stronghold. The ruins of
heir castle stand on the outskirts of the little town, beside
 river, overlooking a valley. Both the castle and valley are
amed in song and story. Moore's verses will occur to you as
you stand in the ivy-clad ruins. You remember the lines, of
course:

> The valley lay smiling before me
> Where lately I left her behind,

> Yet I trembled and something hung o'er me,
>> That saddened the joy of my mind.
> I looked for the lamp which she told me
>> Should shine when her pilgrim returned,
> Yet though darkness began to enfold me,
>> No lamp from the battlement burned.

Well, here you have the valley that lay smiling before him. Here were also the battlements, now no more. They were battered to fragments in the wars of the sixteenth century, but some of the walls remain.

Here Dermod MacMurrough and Dervorgilla, the wife of Tiernan O'Rourke, used to meet. They finally bolted during the absence of O'Rourke, and hence the infamy that has lived on through the ages. When MacMurrough was obliged to fly the country from the vengeance of O'Rourke, he went to England and brought back the Normans. It was a terrible crime, a terrible wrong, a terrible atonement. Mac-Murrough died, falling to pieces, in the pangs of a loathsome disease, and the evil he did lived after him. I am not concerned about his fate at all. But there is some fiction and wasted sympathy mixed up with this tale of Breffni which should be sorted out, so that history may have fair play. For we can do no good by taking our bitter historical pills coated over with the sugar of romance; better swallow them just as they are compounded for us by cold, stern facts. Thomas Moore was no mean historian, but his poetic fancy got the better of him in Dromahair. For example, let us take the lines:

> There was a time, falsest of women,
>> When Brefney's good sword would have sought
> That man through a million of foemen
>> Who dared but to doubt thee in thought.

Here is a splendid and passionate sorrow grandly expressed, but it existed more in the poetic soul of Thomas than in the fierce heart of Tiernan. For Tiernan O'Rourke was no

22

saint. He was just a predatory mountaineer who had a heart as black as the next man. According to the Four Masters, this Tiernan O'Rourke, who, by the way, was called the One-eyed, led his men in 1136 A.D. across the Shannon, on a certain kind of pilgrimage which was little to his credit.

'They raided and sacked Clonard and behaved in so shameless a manner as to strip O'Daly, then chief poet of Ireland. Among other outrages they sacrilegiously took from the vestry of this abbey a sword which had belonged to St Finian, the founder.' The leader of this raid was the person who supposed to be returning from some pious journey when he failed to see Dervorgilla's light on the battlements. He was a nice pilgrim!

Dervorgilla was a 'false one' when she fled, but there are historians who deny that she was 'young'. She was about forty years of age, and was old enough to have sense. She seems to have quickly tired of MacMurrough, or he of her. Anyhow she did not remain with him very long; two years would be the very outside of their criminal relationship after the elopement. She either left him or was left by him, or was taken from him, after which she lived with her people, who were chieftains of Meath.

To give her her due, she seems to have reformed her ways. She built some churches and lived a retired life. It was she who built the beautiful twelfth-century church of the nuns at Clonmacnoise. Thirty-four years after Tiernan O'Rourke had sacked Clonard, the abbey was once more looted in a manner that left even the vandalism of the Breffni men in the shade. The raider this time was O'Rourke's rival, MacMurrough, and he was aided in his ruffianism by Earl Strongbow and the other reavers from over the water.

It is sad to think of, but so is nearly every year of those blood-stained centuries. The ready-handed chieftains raided each other and finished nearly everything that the Danes had left, and it seems we are now beginning to find out that the Danes left a good deal. The Church was the most powerful moral influence in the land, but there was little, if any, real union between it and the State. The State itself was inchoate. Clontarf had left it victorious but inorganic. There were saintly ecclesiastics and there were laymen of statesmanship and patriotism; but neither class had produced a man to fill the leadership left vacant by the death of Brian. The Church had neither the power to protect itself from the blows dealt it by children of its own, nor influence enough to quell the wild passions of the times. The State had neither cohesion nor strength; for the centuries that had gone by since the cursing of Tara had failed to evolve a nation self-centred and self-confident in the practice of well-defined political institutions. Brian of the Tribute would, in all human probability, have given law and order to the whole of Ireland had he survived his victory over the Norsemen. But the fates were unkind, and after the Dane came the Anglo-Norman—and came, alas! to stay. There was no acknowledged and effective leader of the Irish race, no central power, no recognised national government to band the clans together into one solid fighting force and hurl them with crushing strength upon the foe. The invader came upon us in our weakness and we fell a prey to him. And 'through ages of bondage and slaughter' the Church as well as the State was destined to groan beneath the heel of the tyrant, and to look back with futile sorrow to that thrice accursed day when the foundations of centralised civil government were destroyed at Tara by the anger of an all-powerful and over-zealous ecclesiasticism.

And thus it fell out that we passed under the chastening hand of adversity to feel the greatness of our fall, to see the magnitude of our errors, and, in the dark and slow-dragging

24

centuries of oppression and sufferings, to steel and temper our souls, that we may be instinct with all godliness and kingliness when we break at last from the house of bondage and march onward once more towards the greatness of our destinies.

Dromahair is an ideal place to spend a quiet time, far from the roaring crowds of the cities. The railway comes close to the town, but not close enough to be in evidence. It winds in from the Manorhamilton hills and then swings off again across the valleys, and is quickly lost to view. You are within easy reach of busy cities, and yet you seem to be as far away from them as if you were in the heart of a trackless continent. There is no noise, no hurry or worry. No one is interested in your movements. You can stroll along the mountain roads over the hills, and come and go as you wish. No fuss of fashion, no social emulation, no show. Perfect quiet, perfect ease, beautiful scenery, and a hotel—the Abbey Hotel—which is one of the best of its kind in Ireland, and one of the cheapest although its accommodation is first class. It is called after the old Cistercian abbey which stands beyond the town on the river banks.

The ruined abbey shows many traces of its former magnificence. There are three sides of the cloister arches intact, and the beautiful window tracery of the main aisle, over where the high altar stood, is still flawless. It was a very old religious foundation, and the walls now standing were doubtless built to replace the original monastery.

If you have a week or a fortnight to spare you could make Dromahair your headquarters, and take a new route each day for a cycling trip of twenty or thirty miles around. You can see new charms in the country on every journey; and if you begin to long for change of scene, pull out for the north, and a day's spin will take you across the Erne into Donegal.

About two miles from Dromahair, going northward, you skirt a mountain and drop down on the lake shore again. The road runs along the water edge, and over it the scrub-grown hills rise sheer and high into the blue. There are oaks and pines among the hazels, striking their roots as best they can into the clefts of the rocks, and underneath around the gnarled trunks, the mosses and ferns are year by year making a soil. Here is an object lesson in the uses of afforestation which is of great value. It teaches that most of our waste mountain lands could be made productive, and that many a bare hillside in Ireland could be made beautiful by a wood. In Connacht, Ulster and parts of Munster, aye, even in sylvan Leinster, there is room for hundreds of thousands of acres of forest. Irish Ireland should set about planting them at once. It is work for nation builders.

There is one particular hill close to the eastern end of the lake that you ought to climb. It is a stiff piece of work, but the view from the top will repay you. Leave your bicycle on the side of the road which turns off to the right from the shore, and you will find a sort of path through the scrub which will give you your bearings. You cross a piece of sward where the rabbits' tracks are plentiful, after you have made your way through the hazels on the lower slope, and then you come to the sugar-loaf which tops the hills. This is almost perpendicular, but it is covered with hardy bushes by the branches of which you can pull yourself up step by step over the rocks. In a few minutes you are on the summit, looking down in unfeigned admiration on one of the most magnificent lake scenes in the world. The whole length of Lough Gill spreads out beneath your gaze, and you can see far over the hills and along the valleys which encircle it. The splendid perspective is closed by Knock-narea, with the royal cairn which overlooks the picture—a picture fit for kingly eyes. Grey Benbulben frames it to the right, while to the left the purple ridges and sleeping valleys alternate until the sky drops down upon them beyond the distant headwaters of the Shannon.

Right below you is the valley which, according to Moore, lay smiling before Tiernan O'Rourke. It is smiling now, and is certainly fair. It is one of the many valleys that run down to the shore of Lough Gill, all vying with each other in beauty. The big rugged peaks stand guardians over them, and along their green slopes the white-washed farmsteads are set amid the trees.

Tillage field, and meadow, grove and haggard, and pasture, alternate along them until the distance blurs the view. When the mists roll upward from them in the morning and when the gold of the dawn flushes the crags and steals down the heather to the corn fields, it would be a callous nature that would not feel moved. No wonder the people love them so. I stood for a long time gazing on them from near the clouds, with one who could feel their beauty more thoroughly than I.

'It must be awful for any one born here to have to go away and never return!' was what we said as we turned to retrace our steps.

Near the eastern extremity of the lake is a mountain called O'Rourke's Table. You remember the old ballad of 'O'Rourke's Noble Feast'. Well, the top of the mountain yonder is the table on which the feast was set. It is indeed a table fit for such an occasion. It slopes gently from the valley on the far side, but facing the lake it is steep and inaccessible. The solid rock towers aloft on the crest like a huge fortress, and you must, therefore, take it by a flank movement. Unless you care to walk a mile or two round by the chapel, you must climb from near the rocks which front Lough Gill. There is a wood on one side of the mountain, and through this is the safest way. You scramble up through the larches, and then, forcing your way through a dense growth of beautiful ferns, your feet are on the table.

It was a lovely day when two of us stood there, and we shall never forget it. The table is about two miles long and half a mile in width. And such a royal tablecloth! Rich, fragrant, clustering heather! The top of the mountain is covered with peat, and the peat is covered with a growth of heather in which you stand waist high. Rank, sedgy grass and heaps of moss and huge tufts of mountain fern are along the edge near the wood, and right in the centre, where you can look down on the Atlantic and on hundreds of square miles of Ulster and Connacht, as well as Lough Gill, there is moss in which you sink to your knees, and dry clumps of heath in which you could dream your life away. The sedgy beds of broad grass are packed below with dry and withered leaves which yield to your weight as if they were feathers, and crumple as softly under your tread as if they were velvet pile from the old Genoese looms.

You are higher up than the grey peaks of the nearest ranges; you are on a level with others. You are up in the blue air where only the eagle soars and the skylark sings. The rooks and daws and sea fowl are winging their flight below you over lake and valley and hill. Only the clouds lie here when they are lazy or too full of rain to travel. It is the flower of bogs—the canavaun of the mountain tops of Erin!

Not long ago I was reading one of those whimsical articles on the land question by Standish O'Grady—an article written in that vein of gentle, kindly raillery for which the gifted author is noted. He was replying to, or commenting on, some letter in which a correspondent said that 'every man will have his own bit of land when we get compulsory purchase.' 'Then,' said the chieftain, 'I want to file my claim on the Rock of Dunamase.'

He wanted to own (although he is a kind Unionist) the

rock on which Rory O'Moore's fortress stood, the strong-hold from which the Lion of Leix so often swept down in anger on the lordlings of the Pale. Well, there are more people than Standish O'Grady in Ireland who would like to have the fee-simple of Dunamase. I am one of them myself. But I know there are too many prior claims put in, so I shall not file one. No one has, however, yet claimed the Table of O'Rourke, so I am first in the field. It is of little value as an estate. It is only heather and moss and peat and fern and rock. But I covet it all the same.

2

On the Connacht Plains — A Land Laid Desolate — Rath Croghan of Maeve and Dathi — Two Men Raving on a Wall — The Sheep-crooks — The Gentry and the People.

If you wish to study the contemporary situation in Ireland thoroughly, you must make a tour in the great ranch district beyond the Shannon. My voyage of discovery was made by wheel, and it took me over scores and scores of miles of lonely roads, through dust and sunshine and silence, and through six long days of a mid-summer week.

A deep blue summer sky, with patches of fleecy clouds which blotch the bare hillsides with shadows. Grass lands rolling away in long undulating miles to the sky rim, crossed here and there by grassy ridges running from east to west. Along the horizon low ranges of mountains mingle their deep tints with the silvery whiteness of the clouds. Slieve Baun is in the middle distance, to the right, with its twin summits swelling in purple beauty from the plain and fronting the hills of Annaly, a proud and lonely warden of the Shannon.

There are no woodlands, no groves, scarcely any trees at all. There is no agriculture—the fertile desert is uncultivated from end to end. Away from our feet to the crest of the far-off ridges the public road stretches in a straight line across the valley, between the stone walls, breast high, which separate it from the silent fields on either side. On the broad pastures the flocks and herds are scattered, browsing the rich grass which grows over many a usurped hearth. The thin line you see yonder, like the wavy curves of a

30

white ribbon on the grass, is made up of a few score of wethers wending their way down the slope along a path, to the little streamlet in the hollow. A few crows and seagulls wing their flight high up in the blue over the lonesome tracts. They are bound Leinsterwards, where the worm-strewn furrows open in the track of the ploughman attending to the green crops. There is no break in the empty silence save the whimper of the winds. Not a bird voice is upon the air. There is no heather in all this fertile desolation from which the larks might rise in song. There are no copses for the throstles and robins to warble in. Nothing but pasture and sheep and stone walls and the western wind and lone-liness.

Such is the landscape you meet after passing out into the country through the suburbs of Roscommon; such it is until you reach the environs of Boyle. It is a ride of about twenty miles. You may go eastward from Elphin towards Mayo and ride for a whole day through such a scene. You may strike out in a south-westerly direction into Galway and you will find little variety in the landscape. There are vast and unbroken areas of pasture or grazing lands also in Sligo. They are all more or less the same. The land is more fertile in one locality than in another, but it tells the same story everywhere—the story of a land laid desolate.

There has been a great deal of Irish history made on these Connacht uplands, for even in the earliest times, in common with the other great plains of Ireland, they were of considerable importance in the national economy:

> Where the plain of Coman stretches to the dawnlight
> Slopes Cruachain to the sky.

And Cruachain, now called Rath Croghan, was a famous place during the heroic cycles of Erin. It is a noble eminence —it can scarcely be called a hill—which crowns a swelling

31

ridge overlooking the plains of Boyle in the centre of the ranch district. Here was situated the ancient capital of Connacht, and here is also the Rellig-na-Riogh or the royal burial ground. It was here they buried Dathi, the last pagan monarch of Ireland when they brought him home dead on his shield from the Alpine frontiers of ancient Rome, whither he had carried his war against Caesar. His grave is marked by a pillar stone in the cemetery of the kings, around which the bullocks of the ranchers graze in sleek content. Three of the Tuatha de Danaan queens who gave their names to Ireland, Eirie, Fodhla and Banba—were buried at Croghan, together with their husbands. Conn of the Hundred Battles sleeps there, and the cairn of Maeve—the beautiful and wayward and astute—is said to be among the royal tombs.

It was by no dictum of blind chance that Rath Croghan was chosen in the olden time to be the custodian of the throne of Connacht. Neither was Tara chosen at random, nor Kincora, nor Uisnach, nor Alleach, nor any other of the high places of Erin. They were chosen because of the fertility of the district, the beauty of the scenery and the strategetic advantages of position. They afforded splendid pasturage for the royal flocks and herds. In the forests there was game for royal hawk and hound. In the noble streams which swept in long bends through the splendour of the woodlands, there were fish for the royal table, and cool, retired bramble-hidden backwaters where royalty might bathe. And on the level sward below the palaces, or in the forest glades, there were fields for athletic games, and there was room to course the chargers.

Today Rath Croghan, with its royal raths and burial mounds, stands on the naked plain, in the midst of modern grazierdom, and no student of Irish history who is of the Irish race can look upon it unmoved. But it is not alone because its ancient splendour has departed that it makes you sad. Long centuries have passed indeed since Croghan was a word to conjure with in Irish affairs. Its greatness was highest .in the pagan times. But all through the centuries since then, until the accursed days that saw the chains of the Saxon fastened upon Ireland, Croghan was the centre of one of the loveliest and most populous rural districts in the world. It is for the vanished people that the Irish heart is sorrowful as well as for the kingdom that is dead.

Your feelings towards the ancient heroes are mellowed by the glamour of romance. But there is no softening element in the history of yesterday and today as it is written broadly on the landscape. It is for the uptorn homes and the empty fields that you are angry. It is for these things that curses rise to your lips. It is against the infamous law which fomented and sanctioned and authorised the depopulation that you are a rebel to the inmost core of your manhood. And it is for the day that will see English rule swept out of the island, and those plains dotted once more with peaceful, happy, fearing, God-serving, patriotic Irish homes—it is for that blessed day of days that you are hopeful with a yearning, hungry hope.

Think of what it would mean to Ireland if such a rich territory, now given over to sheep and cattle, were divided up into farms of forty or fifty acres each with a family of from five to eight children on each farm! Think of that land with its under-lying, health-giving strata of limestone! The lime in the soil is good for the formation of bones—of sound, thick, massive bones upon which you can grow tough and corded muscle. Think of all the big-boned, deep-chested men and women that you could rear for Ireland where horses and sheep are now being prepared for export to the armies and stomachs of foreigners.

The evil of depopulation is a tragic and maddening phase of the land question which meets you on nearly every road in Ireland. Depopulation of the most fertile land, synchronised with the crowding together of the people upon the bogs and moors and mountain sides. In no country except Ireland would this have been tolerated without a struggle that would have aroused the world. Blood would have been shed in torrents over it. Blood has been shed in Ireland on account of it, but not in torrents—only in thin driblets. Landlords and their minions have occasionally fallen under the vengeance of their victims, and the English Press has shrieked in Pharasaical horror, calling the Irish peasantry cut-throats and barbarians. But no country in the civilised world would have tolerated a worthless feudalism so long. It would have goaded any other people into action, tempestuous, and sanguinary, and devastating. Were it not that the Irish people have been so obedient to moral restraint, the lives of rackrenting landlords would not have been worth a farthing many a time during the nineteenth century. In other countries famine and despair and exasperation have waded knee deep in the life blood of oppression, leaving to the moralists and historians the task of weighing and fixing responsibility. Our patience and fortitude in Ireland are glorified as heroic Christian virtues. And such indeed they are. But, by Heaven, if there is one thing more than another a thoughtful Irishman is tempted to regret when contemplating the tragedy of our history it is that our capacity for moral endurance was at times so great and that our spirit of active resistance to tyranny was not ten thousand times greater!

Some such thought as this must have been in the minds of two men who sat on a wall by a Connacht roadside scowling upon a magnificent sweep of country wherein not a dozen homes were visible in all the wide miles of lucious grass.

'Do you know what?' said one to the other, waving his

34

hand towards Rath Croghan, which loomed against the cloudless sky in the sunny distance. 'I wish I had some of the power that was centred yonder when Ferdiah and his companions went out against the Red Branch.'

'What would you do with it?' asked the other. And the first speaker promptly answered.

'To begin with, a man could give grazierdom and its patrons a surprise. It would be worth a year of my life to scoop up all the livestock from these Connacht plains.'

'A border raider—a stock lifter! Is that what you would make of yourself?' said the other, shaking his head. 'Has history no lesson for you? Did not Maeve live to bewail her raid for the Red Bull of Ulster?'

'There is no parallel between my little dream,' said the dreamer, 'and the old legend which you recall, for I would drive the flocks and herds northward through the Ulster passes to be slaughtered to feed an Irish army that had at last shaken out the war flag. No doubt you will say I am raving, but I am not so bad as that. I am laying down what, under conceivably fortuitous circumstances, might be a practical and attractive military proposition. Do you follow me?'

The other was a man of peace and a man of God; but he smote his knee and threw up his head.

'My hand to you!' he cried, in the dear delight of caressing the wild and witching ideal which had burst into his peaceful life. 'It would be splendid! To clear out the Connacht plains! It would be a terrible haul. Why, listen to me, it would feed 40,000 men for months! I read somewhere the other day that there are sheep and cattle enough west of the Shannon to feed Ireland during a blockade of years.'

'As a matter of authenticated history,' remarked his companion, 'there was as much food exported from Ireland to England during the famine as would sustain the entire population of the country.'

'And we let it go!' commented the other, in a tone widely at variance with his peaceful calling. 'It is a lesson for the future which Ireland should remember.'

'So you are one of those who have faith in the future?' asked the dreamer.

'I am,' was the proud reply,'even if the present were ten times blacker than it is, even if our past were ten times more tragic. I look forward to a time when the rule of the outlander shall be no more in Ireland, and when the dark shadow cast by his presence on the land shall have given place to the sunshine of freedom. But say, am I raving any way well?'

'Splendidly! Go ahead!' cried the dreamer, encouragingly.

'Ah, if all the raving we do were only half a prophecy!' he continued with a smile, half sad, half playful. 'If even our tamest dreams came true, what a grand thing it would be. Think of how joyful it would be, when the fight was ended, to see the people shifting their homes out of the bogs and settling down again here on these plains, where their race has lived for ages. There would have to be strict legislation about it, of course, and commissioners to examine and decide regarding claims and all that. And there would be a board to look after afforestation, so that stately groves and woods should in time again beautify the land.'

And for half an hour and more the two Irishmen sat there on the wall in the rapture of a proud delirium, weaving patriotic fancies amidst the Connacht desolation.

It is not easy to give an adequate idea of depopulation as it exists. I had no adequate idea of it myself until I saw it. I stood by the pillar stone over King Dathi's grave on Rath Croghan and looked over the grasslands which spread around me for miles. I could see at least three or four leagues in every direction. I can safely affirm that there was not one house to the square mile. I walked hither and thither around the burial mounds, and examined the subjacent plains from various points of view, and at no time could I count a dozen houses.

The richness of the soil was evidenced in many ways. There could be no doubt that the land was some of the best in Europe. It could easily support in decent and prosperous comfort a family to every fifty acres—families that could give higher education to their boys and dowries to their girls. If there were a family to every fifty acres those plains would have a population of thousands and thousands. At present there are tracts of the Pampas more thickly peopled. And there is ample room on the Connacht ranches for all the emigrants that ever left Ireland for the great stock runs of the South.

During my tour I fell in with one of the parish priests of the diocese of Elphin, who said: 'I have 110 sheep crooks in my parish,' meaning that instead of hundreds of agriculturist families, he had 110 herdsmen. Another sagart with whom I had the pleasure of conversing told me that he had spent all the years of his mission on the Connacht plains. He said that in his own parish at that present moment two-thirds of the congregation were shepherds. The other third consisted of unfortunate people who were living on the skirt of the plains in little holdings which they had themselves reclaimed from the bogs and moors and swamps, and for which they had been rackrented in proportion to the extent of the improvements effected by their own labour.

And let us not forget that the people crowded together on the skirts of the plains—on the bogs and moors and mountains—starved in body and mind, bent by toil and chilled by penury, are the rightful owners of the ranches. They are the descendants of the clansmen who held the land under the chieftains. They are the people who were

37

hounded out of their rights under the laws which English domination imposed upon the country. They are the descendants of the men who were dispossessed so that the soil might be portioned out among the soldiers who had fought for the conquest of the nation. They are the tenants who were evicted by the sheep and cattle breeders.

During my cycling tours through Connacht I have in various places come across the work of the Congested Districts Board. The Board buys any grazing property or other tract of unoccupied land which comes within the possibilities of its financial resources. It then drains, fences, and lays out the land into farms of from twenty to thirty acres each, and the men who are paid for doing this work are from the locality, and are generally the people who will be the new tenants. Comfortable but plain and suitable dwellings are then erected, with out-offices, etc., and the farms are then ready for the occupiers.

The Board is slow in its operations, and it is able to cope with only a very small part of the work to be done. But it is, with all its drawbacks, a move which commends itself to approval and justification by the results already accomplished. And it points the way to the definite solution of the Irish land question. That solution has not been given by the Land Act of 1903. If has merely been played with. The question has been begged, while the price of land has been inflated. The solution of the Irish land question cannot be achieved by half measures. It is a deeply seated evil and needs a drastic remedy. Landlordism will have to go, root and branch, with all its sporting rights and turbary rights and head rents and mining royalties, and every other feudal and archaic absurdity. Compulsory sale, and nothing less, is the only remedy, and come it must soon or late.

I crossed the River Suck south of the little town of Athleague and struck westward into Galway, never halting till I came to Mount Bellew. Here I visited the schools and college established by the Franciscan Brothers many years ago. The institution is now known as the College of Saint Francis, and is one of the foremost educational establishments in the West. It is, in every sense of the word, an Irish college, and makes a speciality of the Irish language.

I met the Rev. Brother Superior of the Franciscan teachers at the College of Saint Francis and had the pleasure of a long conversation with him. When he spoke of the other houses of the Brothers in Connacht, and of the work still to be done in Ireland for God and country, you saw at once the fine spirit of this faithful body of Irishmen—modest, simple, practical men of the people who have done so much in the cause of Irish education.

Ah, me! one cannot help wasting thought in poor Ireland on the Might Have Been! And, while in the College of Mount Bellew, I could not help thinking of the fight of stout old John of Tuam against the denationalising schools of which Whately was the apostle. If the Lion of Saint Jarlath's had gained his point when the misnamed national education system was projected, and if Ireland for the past forty years and more had been taught by men like the Franciscan Brothers, there would be little need today for the propaganda of the Gaelic League. Archbishop MacHale stood for a total rejection of the national schools, and said that the children of Ireland should be educated on Irish lines. A temporising policy was substituted for this wise and manly ideal; and from the day on which this melancholy error was committed the Aglicisation of the Irish mind went on apace.

In Connacht, as indeed in the other provinces of Ireland, speaking generally, the old-time friendly relations which in many instances existed between the classes and the masses are passing away. That those friendly relations have not entirely disappeared is due to the rational and patriotic stand taken by a few of the gentry who have departed from the cast-iron traditions of landlordism and thrown in their lot with the people. It would be better for their class and for Ireland if their example were extensively followed; but Ireland and the Irish people will struggle along without the men who, after all, are standing more in their own light than in the light of the nation.

The Land Acts already won by the people, meagre and shuffling though they are, have still written on the wall the doom of the landlord oligarchy in Ireland. Compulsory sale will sound the death knell of the ascendancy, and after that the fittest will survive. Any class or clique which persists in the belief that it has separate interests from the Irish people will go to the wall. The class known as the gentry of Ireland —or, to be more accurate, 'the nobility and gentry'—believe they have separate interests from the people upon whom they live. Consequently they will not survive. Standish O'Grady, one of themselves, and one of the best of them, told them the truth when he said that they were going, going—'rotting from the land, without one brave deed, without one brave word.' It is a terrible epitaph to write over the grave of a caste that might have been the glory and the salvation of the country. But it is true, and to none is this truth more sad and appealing than to Standish O'Grady himself, the knightly Irish gentleman who gave it utterance.

It was during my cycling tour west of the Shannon that this decay of the Irish gentry was brought most vividly home to me. I think I ought to tell you about it, and in doing so I will ask you to be kind enough to let me unfold the tale in my own way.

I was riding with an Irish Irelander through one of the rare wooded spots in the great ranch district when a few glimpses of the demesne by which we were passing, caught through gaps in the crumbling walls along the wayside, caused me to suggest a halt. On every side were signs of fallen fortunes, of neglect and poverty and ruin. The park was evidently a vast rabbit warren and the sward was over-run with whins. The groves were wide tangles of under-bush. The grand avenue was grass-grown and mossy. The 'big house' itself still made a brave show, but the out-offices were woefully dilapidated. Under some of the giant elms and beeches to the rear of the mansion the bare gables of a ruined kennel showed where the foxhounds had once fed and yelped and slept. The lodge at the grand gate was un-tenanted and neglected. The gate itself was rickety, and swung half open on its crazy hinges.

'Who lives here?' I asked, wishing to know the name of the person or persons whose residence had seen better days, and on whose property the symptoms of consumption were so conspicuous and unmistakable.

'A member of the Broken Down,' replied my comrade, mentioning a name which there is no need to repeat. 'They were great people once, but times have changed for them, and, as you see, they are aground on the shoals of adversity.'

'What do they live on?'

'Rabbits, principally, and three-weeks-old illustrated papers sent to them more or less irregularly by some wealthy connections who live in London.'

'And are the people of their own class in the country round about so unkind as to leave them here in the pangs of genteel famine?'

'What can be expected of folks who are more or less in the same financial straits themselves? It's nearly six of one and half a dozen of the other. They are all hard up. If it weren't for their pride and lack of brains they'd be dead long ago. Their pride keeps the best side out, and their lack of brains prevents them from understanding the emptiness and fatuity of their lives.'

'What evil spirit took charge of their destiny, I wonder?'

'Various evil spirits,' explained the Irish Irelander. 'The evil spirit of denationalisation that led them into a slough of stupid imitation and make-believe in which nothing can thrive; the evil spirit of snobbery which made them live above their means; the evil spirit of pride which would not allow them to throw in their lot with that of the common people; and besides these evil spirits, there were the devils of drink and gambling and lust.

3

On all the roads between Banagher and Athlone there are troops of people facing westward. They are on vehicles of every kind, from the dashing excursion brake to the humble donkey cart, and every kind of bicycle procurable is also in evidence. Hundreds of people are tramping the roads in the dust, hundreds are footing it over the fields and hills; and there are many boats on the Shannon, all laden to the very gunwales with people from Connacht. And whether the crowds come out of Westmeath or western Offaly, or from Galway or Roscommon, they are all converging in a common destination; they are all on the way to Clonmacnoise of the Seven Churches. For this is the Sunday morning nearest to 9 September, the feast of St Ciaran (or Kieran). It is 'pattern' or patron day—a day of prayer, or penance, and cheery festivity, too, and courtship and laughter and dancing—a day made up of Irish faith and Irish history, revealed in the softer lights of Irish character. I am going to the 'pattern' myself, and I am taking the reader with me, if there is no objection.

Two round towers, a wilderness of crumbling walls and naked gables, a forest of tombstones, and the wide river

43

flowing peacefully through the callows which are studded with haycocks up to the very boundary of the cemetery. That is Clonmacnoise as we first catch sight of it from the Cloghan road.

There is a long, low range of grassy hills between the bog and the river, and on the western slope of this ridge, just where the Shannon makes one of its magnificent loops, St Ciaran founded his little oratory on 23 January, A.D. 544. Ciaran died in a few months afterwards, but his oratory—the Eclais Beg—developed into a great seat of piety and learning, was surrounded in course of time by a populous city, and its name spread throughout Europe, from nearly every country of which scholars flocked to its schools and university.

The holy place which we are approaching by the hilly roads that wind past the farmsteads of Clonfanlough is in ruins, for it has seen stormy times and it is very old. It was old before the Saracens were smashed at Tours, before Norman William landed at Hastings, before the Crusades were preached or fought. It was old before many of the present great universities of Christendom were founded, and before any of the present royal families of Europe were heard of in authentic history. It was old when the Danes raided its cloisters. It had celebrated the eleven hundredth anniversary of its foundation before the sacrilegious soldiery of Elizabeth reduced it to ruin. It flourished in the golden age of Christian Erin, and it received and holds the mortal remains of the last of the Irish kings. All this is down in history; and it is written on the grey walls and tombs and monuments of the Seven Churches here beside the Shannon.

Let us enter the ruins. Tread lightly on the graves which crowd the sward, for some of the noblest and loveliest and purest and greatest that Ireland has seen are sleeping here. This thought is assuredly present in the minds of those men and women who are praying in groups here and there. See, they have taken off their boots and stockings, and are going barefoot over the holy ground. They go round the graves of the saints on their knees. They kiss the floors of the churches. They tell their beads below the great sculptured cross in front of the Dananlaig or Tempull McDermott. They go bareheaded along the causeway to the old nunnery of Dervorgilla. They cross themselves before drinking from the blessed wells. They whisper pious invocations as they drop hairpins or buttons or matches or pebbles into the niches and cavities where toothaches, headaches, warts and other ills are left behind.

Here you have a husband and wife from beyond the Shannon who have come fasting for miles to 'do the stations' and perform all the traditional devotions of the day. They are bareheaded and their feet are bare and red from the scratches of briars and the stings of nettles. They are kneeling on the damp grass in front of the small cross now, and the man is giving out the Lord's Prayer in Irish. The woman gives the responses in Irish also. How soft and sweet the words are! What piety and supplication are in the cadences! How appropriate is the old language on their lips in prayer this day and in this place! It is not only an echo of the past. It is the continuity of tradition. It is the tongue that was on Ciaran's lips when he preached and taught and prayed. It is the tongue in which the sages of Clonmacnoise lectured and wrote. It is the soul's voice of Holy Ireland— the treasure house in which her heart is guarded from the pollution of the rotting world.

Here at the entrance to Tempull McDermott is the Whispering Arch. The moundings of the arch are so deep and well preserved that they carry a whisper from one side of the doorway to the other. There is a youth from near Shannonbridge standing on one side of the door with his

45

mouth close to the mouldings. On the other side, with her back turned towards him, is a maiden from near Banagher, blushing at the amorous nonsense which the swain from Shannonbridge is whispering.

It is a dalliance like unto that which is carried on by conversation lozenges. Two of the girl's friends draw near and put their ears to the moulding. They giggle and blush and say 'Oh, d'ye hear that?' and they say things back to the youth from Shannonbridge, who opens his face in a festive grin or looks sheepish, according as the message received is sympathetic or caustic. He is joined by two other youths of the party, and they guffaw and punch one another in the ribs and whisper more or less profoundly original inanities into the hard worked old arch which a forbearing Providence keeps from falling down and crushing them. This whispering has been going on for generations—aye, for ages. In the graveyard is the dust of men and women who made love there at the doorway, as these youngsters are now doing; and the young people of the future will do the same no doubt.

The Whispering Arch is not as old as the church. It dates from the fourteenth or fifteenth century. The church was repaired or rebuilt by Tomaltach McDermott, Chieftain of Moylurg, some time about 1320 or 1330. Hence the church is called Tempull McDermott. It was originally built in A.D. 909 by Flann, King of Ireland and by Colman, Abbot of Clonmacnoise.

It was to commemorate the building of the church, and also to mark the grave of King Flann that the great cross was erected. This is Petrie's opinion, an opinion shared by Bishop Healy and also by Dean Monahan, the learned author of the 'Records of Clonmacnoise'. The Great Cross of Clonmacnoise is hewn from the solid limestone in the Celtic style of pannelled statues and interlaced tracery.

On every 'pattern' day it is the centre of a crowd of

visitors. Not only do many of the pilgrims pray around it, but many of the men try to span its shaft with their arms. Anyone who is able to meet the tips of his fingers around the shaft is believed to have certain powers conferred upon him by virtue of which he is enabled to save human life in certain given circumstances. Hence it is that so many men of all classes and ages are anxious to span the cross; and hence it is also that their friends are anxious for them to succeed. There goes a young husband to span it, but the tips of his fingers are still a good half inch apart. There are two sturdy pilgrims praying at the base of the cross and to them the wife appeals: 'Give him a hand to span it, and God bless you,' she says. They are on their feet in a twinkling of your eye, and one of them climbs up on the base of the cross in front, and the other climbs up behind. The one in front catches the husband's fingers and pulls the man's arms further round the shaft. The one behind shoves the candidate between the shoulders and crushes his breast. thus aided and stretched and tortured, the young husband's fingers meet around the shaft, and with arms benumbed and a bruised and aching breastbone, he thanks the pilgrims and returns to his wife, who is smiling with pride and happiness. Nothing can terrify her now. Her life is safe. Her husband has spanned the big cross of the Seven Churches! She says 'God bless you' again to the obliging pilgrims, but they have resumed their prayers, and another man is already throwing his arms around the sculptured panels of the *Cros na Scraeptra*, as the cross is sometimes called.

He is a low sized man—this new competitor for the honour—and he would need two or three inches more on each arm before he could even hope for success. But he is desperately in earnest, and so persevering, and his inability to span the shaft so manifest that the crowd laughs heartily. He strains and stretches and gets red in the face, and asks

47

for help; and this provokes more laughter. If he is to span that shaft he will have to be pulled to pieces first and made into a rope. At length he gives in, and very crestfallen descends to earth again, quivering from muscular exertion and excitement and bathed in perspiration.

Another takes his place, a young giant, lean of chest and long of arm. Without aid from anyone and without making any extraordinary effort he meets his hands round the shaft and the crowd applauds. Then there is a long chorus of enquiries.

Whence this man? Who is he that has spanned the cross? Where does he live? He is a man of mark now. Some winter's night, months hence, he may be called out of his warm bed and requested for God and Mary's sake to go off miles and miles, through the frost and bitter wind, in order to span a sufferer who is in danger of death. It is to find out his name and address that so many people are enquiring about him now; and he, the hero of the hour, blushes and smiles modestly as he retires; for he is a mere youth and a stranger here, and it is only now that he has been told all that spanning the *Cros na Scraeptra* involves. Others take his place on the stone plinth, and the spanning trials go on and on as they have done on every 'pattern' day for centuries.

In the middle of the grounds is the little oratory of St Ciaran—the Eclais Beg. In the long ago it was, as it is now, the 'centre of the holiness of Clonmacnoise'. But it is not the oratory that Ciaran built. The original structure must have been of wood or wattle and clay. But the present ruin occupies the exact site of the cell of St Ciaran. The saint's grave is supposed to be beside it. Other saints are buried within. The general voice of local tradition says that St Ciaran's grave is outside the walls of the Eclais Beg—on the side near the Shannon. But many people are uncertain about this point.

Do you see these men and women who are scooping up handfuls of clay from under the stones? They are going to take that clay home with them—and they are going to take it with a simple unshaken and unshakable faith which surprises what people call philosophy in this sceptical age. What are they going to do with it? Ask them. To banish red worms that eat the oats. To sprinkle on the floors of houses where sickness abides. There are scores of people here who will tell you of rescued crops and resweetened pastures and banished infection due to this miracle working clay gathered by the graveside of St Ciaran.

And at the saint's well beside the Shannonbridge road, down the fields yonder, you will find people taking away bottles of water to cure aches and pains. You will find others drinking, for a like purpose from St Finian's well, beside the Shannon, as you go to the old nunnery.

On the western boundary of the churchyard is Tempull Finian, which was built probably in the ninth century and dedicated to St Finian, the great prelate of Clonard. The chancel arch of this church is considered to be one of the finest specimens extant of Celtic Romanesque. There is a round tower attached to this church which is complete and perfect. It is a small tower, being only fifty-six feet high.

Tempull Connor was founded by Cathal, son of Conchobar. But it does not seem likely that King Rodrick was buried in this church. His grave, according to the antiquarians and local tradition, is beside the high altar of the great church of Tempull McDermott. Some of the MacCoughlans, chief of Delvin Ara, are buried in the same place, I think.

Near the Eclais Beg is Tempull Kelly, built by Connor O'Kelly, one of the Chiefs of Hy-Many. On the other side of the great church is Tempull Righ—the King's church, built by the southern branch of the Hy-Niall in memory of King Diarmuid. Tempull Hurpan, in front of which stands the smaller cross, stands to the right of Tempull McDermott. O'Rourke's round tower stands at the north-western corner of the cemetery. The 'Registry of Clonmacnoise' says it was built by Fergal O'Rourke of Breffni, King of Connacht, towards the middle of the tenth century. O'Rourke, we are told, built this tower, and kept the churches of Clonmacnoise in repair during his life, for his soul's sake, and as the price of his family sepulchre in the holy ground of Ciaran. But is this account of the building correct? It may well be doubted.

These towers seem to have nothing in common with the other pieces of masonry. The very materials are different. The tower, which stands on the corner of the ruined church of St Finian, was certainly not built at the same time as the church. Its side was grooved in a slanting direction to admit the roof of the building.

When Ireland has schooled herself to go back to the honouring of mere Irish saints the name of Ciaran will stand out as one of the greatest in the history of the Church. In Irish hagiology he is usually called Ciaran Mac-in-Tsair—the son of the carpenter—and sometimes Ciaran the younger, to distinguish him from St Ciaran of Saigher, the patron of Ossory. His father, although a tradesman, was of noble lineage. They claim his birthplace for Roscommon, and also for Westmeath. He was baptised in A.D. 512, doubtless the year of his birth. He received his education at Clonard, and there made the acquaintance of the holy men who were afterwards known as the Twelve Apostles of Erin. St Finian was his master.

When he left Clonard he went to Aran where he worked with St Enda. Then he was on Scattery Island in the Lower Shannon for a time. From there he went to Hare Island, in Lough Ree, where he founded an oratory, the ruins of which are still be be seen. He also founded an oratory at

Athlone. From Hare Island he went further down the Shannon and founded another oratory; but the land around it was too fertile for a man who had made a vow of holy poverty, and so he went on to Ard Tipratt—the Hill or Height of the Spring, afterwards called Clonmacnoise.

The word Clonmacnoise, according to John O'Mahony's note on page 94 of his translation of Keating, comes from Cluain-MacNois, signifying 'the retreat of the sons of the noble', either from the great numbers of the sons of the Irish nobility who resorted to its college for education, or from many of the Irish princes having burial places in its cemetery. Joyce says it means 'the meadow of the Son of Nos'. The Four Masters call it by this same name practically. St Ciaran took only four months to build his Eclais Beg. The following legend regarding the founding of Clonmacnoise is told in the 'Chronicon Scotrum', and also in the 'Leabhar Buidhe Lecain'.

When Ciaran was planting the first post to mark out the ground at Clonmacnoise, Diarmuid MacCearbhaill, a young prince who was a fugitive in the district, helped the saint with his own hands to drive the pole into the ground. 'Though your companions today are few,' said Ciaran, 'tomorrow thou shalt be High King of Erin.' One of Diarmuid's companions was Maelmor, his foster brother, and, hearing the prophecy, this man went and slew King Tuathal Maelgarbh, great grandson of Niall the Great, who had set a price on Diarmuid's head. The men from Tara and Meath then sought out Diarmuid, who was the true heir to the Ardrighship, and proclaimed him High King of Erin. On the Great Cross in front of Tempull McDermott the saint and the king are represented on one of the sculptured panels with their hands on a pole in commemoration of the founding of Clonmacnoise.

Diarmuid ascended the throne of Tara in A.D. 544. It

was during his reign that Tara was cursed by St Ruadhan of Lorrha. Soon after the curse was pronounced Tara was deserted.*

St Ciaran lived only four months after founding his monastery. He died at the sacred age of thirty-three in his Eclais Beg, and near the very spot where his ashes are said to rest. His bosom friend, St Kevin, of Glendalough, was with him to the end. His death was a tremendous loss to Ireland. Had he lived, the influence which he exercised in the councils of the Church would have kept the other bishops of Ireland from making war upon Tara. Thus, King Diarmuid would have been free to enforce the laws, to quell the wild insubordination of the petty kings, and to lay securely and broadly the foundations of the State. Had this been done the Norsemen would have found Ireland a strong and united nation. And as for the Anglo-Normans, they would never have dreamt of attacking a people whose institutions of civil government had been sufficiently developed to place the combined and ordered force of the nation at the service of the nation's need.

Here is the ruin known as 'Devorgilla's Nunnery'. She was the wife of Tiernan O'Rourke of Breffni, who eloped with MacMurrough. She repented of her sin and separated from her paramour after two years, as we have seen in another chapter, to spend the rest of her life doing good works. This is one of the convents she built. The doorway of the chapel is still beautiful. It was repaired some years ago. It is of the flat-arched Norman school, which would in time have developed into a style distinctly Irish. Even as it is there is a distinctiveness about it which is worthy of close

*One of the deepest students of Irish history in our day wrote to me as follows: 'I do not believe a word about the cursing of Tara. It is an invention of the century.'

study. It marks undoubtedly the beginning of a school of architectural design which had many splendid possibilities.

Have you noticed how Clonmacnoise brackets two Irish names fraught with tragic significance—Diarmuid and Devorgilla? Diarmuid lived centuries before Devorgilla, and was of a character quite different to that of the faithless wife of Dromahair. But connected with each of their names, although for widely different reasons, there is a chapter of history crowded with the ruin of Ireland.

At the nunnery ruins there is laughter and some quiet match-making. Under the twelfth century arches there are flirtations going on, for it is now late in the afternoon. At four o'clock this morning when the sky was barely grey over the Shannon, pilgrims crept under those very arches on bare knees. Peradventure some of those pilgrims are here now on another quest. It is quite possible. There is all that and something more in this Irish nature of ours.

Beside the ancient causeway which leads from the nunnery to the church there are many luncheon and tea parties; and they are all gay. Chickens, ducks, sandwiches, bread and butter, and bottled stout are in great plenty, and in great demand. And you hear the popping of lemonade and soda water corks, and the rattle of teacups, and the laughter which rises above the animated talk.

Here is a man with a cornet, which he can play splendidly. Listen! there goes the 'Coulin', played exquisitely. He is a character is this strolling musician, and he is utterly forgetful of the dancers who pound the green sward with the weight of solid flesh and bone and shoe leather, manufactured let us hope, in Ireland.

Here are two pairs of lovers seated on a mossy bank beside the silent river, and it is evident that Cupid has his hands full. They are sitting on ground over which hundreds of people are coming and going, but they have eyes and ears

53

only for each other. The folk who have kindness in their hearts for everything that is human, regard them with a passing smile of comprehension and tolerant benevolence. But the majority of the pilgrims look upon them with calm amusement. No one wonders at them. No one questions their right to be there. No one is shocked or scandalised. One buxom matron with the red petticoat and dark cape and snow-white cap of the trans-Shannon women nods her head approvingly at them and gives them a friendly word in Irish, which a man beside me translated as: 'Bless you, my children four.' And let us say amen to that by all means, and hope that they may live happy forever after. See in each idyll around us, my brothers, the triumph of life and love over death. In the graveyard—even over the bones of the dead—even where death may lay claim to a victory— Love laughs and takes his own—takes it smilingly, and joyously holds out his hands to the future—proudly conscious that nothing avails against his sway over the continuity of life.

There are tents beside the narrow road leading from the cemetery to the highway. There are apple carts, ginger bread carts, shooting galleries, and other enterprises, sporting and commercial. We make our way through them and gain the open fields beside the Shannon. The day has flown quickly, and the feast is over now. The rest is soon told.

A snack of cold fowl, a smoke, a pleasant chat in the shadow of the old castle built by John de Gray at some distance from the churches. A stroll back to the cars. A glorious drive along the hill crests in the sunset splendour. Then the fading shadows and the brightening of the moon and the cool sweetness of the twilight. Miles of level road through meadows and under autumn woods and past fields where the yellow corn drank the falling dew. Through the villages where the windows flashed bravely, and where the kitchen fires gleamed over the neat half-doors. Bowling home with the hoof strokes ringing on the gravel, and the wheels flinging back the moonbeams. Oh, it was grand—grand—grand!

4

The Valley of the Lower Shannon — From Aughrim to Limerick — Mountain and Lowland Children — The Rim of the World — Nenagh Town — Dairy Farming — The Unharnessed, Idle, Beautiful Shannon — An Exclusive Bodach — Upholding First Principles — Killaloe — Ancient Kincora — Brian and Mahon — Castleconnell Rapids — Limerick in the Gloaming.

I had cycled from Kilcommedan Hill eastward, crossing the Shannon at Banagher, and thence striking southward until I reached a place below Meelick, near Redwood. Kilcommedan Hill is another name for the battlefield of Aughrim. Redwood is the place where Donal O'Sullivan crossed into Connacht from Munster on his retreat after the Battle of Kinsale. I had been in the track of De Ginkell's march to Galway, and had been exploring the country where St Ruth elected to make his stand against the Dutch general. I had also been picking up the route of O'Sullivan Beare on the slopes of Aughrim, where he had fought and routed a jackal horde that had tried to stop him. I halted now on the Munster plain, and considered whether I had enough of history for one day, or whether I should push forward towards Limerick. My home under the blue Slieve Blooms lay only about ten miles to the eastward, and 'the City of the Violated Treaty' lay many miles to the southward. But the day was young and the roads were good, and the wind for a wonder came out of the north-east, and would help me on a southerly ride. It was a long ride I mapped out for myself, as I sat on a stone beside a spring which flowed out into the sunlight through the moss-grown roots of a haw-thorn and danced and sang over the pebbles, and down hill, falling into silence as it stole out of sight amongst the tempting watercresses. I finished a bunch of cress, slaked my thirst once more in the laughing shallows, and after a final look at my road map, concentrated on Borrisokane to begin with. After that my route would bring me into touch with the country of Brian Boru and Sarsfield and Galloping O'Hogan and Garryowen and the Wild Geese.

To the children in the country of the O'Carroll's, north of Birr, the far-away mountains below Nenagh make the southern limit of the world. All through my childhood the dim peaks of the Silvermines and the Keepers seemed to be infinitely distant, and when as a boy I learned that there were other countries besides the one which lay between me and the horizon, I often longed to see them, and often wondered if it would be my fate to travel in the regions beyond the guardian hills of the homeland. I suppose all this is in the childhood and boyhood of most people born in the valleys. I have never been able to find out what theories of the universe float through the minds of Irish children born on the mountains. I tried to coax this secret out of mountain children here and there through Ireland, but they baffled me. They seemed to have no idea at all that they were of the hills themselves. Any heather-clad peak above them was 'the mountain', but the slopes of the range upon which they had been born did not strike them as being big, purple, beautiful mysterious things to the children of the plains and vales.

'What is down there, do you suppose?' I asked a little boy whom I met on a mountain slope over southern Ulster.

'Down where?' he said, with a look which told me he did not understand.

I made a gesture which included most of Cavan and

Leitrim.

'Why, that isn't down there,' he said, with a smile.

'And what is it?' I asked.

'Oh! its over there beyond, that's what we say,' he replied, and beyond that I could not induce him to go.

But when I fell in with a party of schoolchildren on the road south of Borrisokane, and asked them what lay beyond the Keepers, they could tell me that it was Limerick. And when I asked them, pointing to the north-east, what lay beyond the Slieve Blooms, they could tell me that it was Queen's County. They were children of the plains, and from the time they could walk they had been questioning the mountains.

'I am going to the other side of the Silvermines, and away beyond the Keepers,' I said, 'and maybe any of you would like to come?'

There was silence for a few seconds, and then a brown-haired lad asked shyly, as he made crosses with his toes in the road dust:

'Are you goin' as far as Limerick?'

'I am, and much farther,' I said — 'miles and miles!— going even farther than the coast of Ireland—going over the sea—Will you come?'

He shook his head and smiled. But as I left them there was a wistful light in his eyes and in the eyes of more than one of his companions. And I knew that some Hy-Brazil of their own creation had come into 'the long, long thoughts of youth'. It was my own boyhood back again. The same dumb questioning—the same inarticulate longings—the same subconscious desire to learn what is out there beyond the blue and purple, and to see it, and feel upon your cheek, and hear in your ears the breath and voice of the world.

I found Nenagh very quiet, and left it so. I drank cider, and smoked a pipe, and read the papers, and looked an inquisitive policeman out of countenance. The town appears to be prosperous. There is a fine rich country around it, but not a great deal of agriculture. Dairy farming seems to be the principal industry thereabouts, and also beyond the mountains, on the plains of Limerick. The farms do not, however, run into big acreages. I passed through various districts where a holding of over fifty acres was the exception. The average size of a farm appeared to be somewhere between twenty-five and thirty acres. The land, although under pasture, was not therefore empty of people. Dairy farming requires more hands than grazing. It means that there must be a family at least, or, if not, two or three paid hands to milk the cows, handle the milk, and feed the calves. Butter making at home on the farm has become practically a thing of the past in most dairy farming districts. The milk is collected by vans and carried to a local creamery, where the cream is taken from it by means of mechanical separators. Next day the skim-milk is taken away by the farmers, or sent back to them. The cream is then sent to Limerick, or some other central place, and made into butter. There is at times a good deal of discussion as to the best means of working a co-operative dairy system. Opinions are very much divided at times regarding matters of detail; but as a rule it is conceded by the farmers that the general principle of co-operation is fraught with encouraging possibilities.

Nenagh, like Clonmel, was a more prosperous town in the great days of the Irish corn trade than now. I was surprised to find that the impulse of the Irish-Ireland movement has been felt far less in Tipperary than in counties which might be supposed to be less Irish. But a force of the right kind is working slowly but surely, and a change is coming. In the towns of Tipperary, as in the towns of most of the other Irish counties, there are merchants who regard it as their duty to sell Irish manufactured goods, and, if necessary recommend them to their customers; and in the rural districts the farmers are waking up to the conviction that their duties towards the Irish nation did not end, but in a manner only really began, with the partial settlement of the land question. In order to foster Irish industries some kind of Protection is necessary. Circumstanced as she is at present—governed as she is by England in the selfish commercial and political interest of England—Ireland is unable to make Protection the law of the land in a legal sense. But she is already beginning to do it in a moral sense; 'Burn everything English but English coal' is a saying that was for many years dead in a sleepy and forgetful Ireland. But it has been resuscitated of late, and the fiscal policy of which it is, of course, a picturesque apothegm, coined in the wondrous mind of Swift, is coming into play. The Irish people are learning that every time they buy even a box of matches of Irish manufacture in preference to any other, they are striking a blow for Ireland. It is the policy of moral protection. There is no law of England which obliges Irishmen under penalties and pains to favour English manufactures and boycott their own. And a re-awakening Ireland is taking a firm grasp of this economic fact and of all that it means.

I turned westward in Nenagh, and picked up the Shannon once more at Portroe, where Lough Derg narrows into a long strip of water, not more than a mile in width, bordered on the Clare side by the wooded hills which rise into the Bernagh range. The Tipperary side is relatively flat, but very picturesque; and from this point to Killaloe the Shannon is indeed lordly. But it is, unfortunately, an empty, profitless lordship. It is not the lordship of the Rhine or the Rhone or the Danube. It is devoid of the traffic of commerce. The magnificent river is not a factor in the national economy.

Its potentialities are asleep. The Shannon is mighty, but idle.

There is a little island in Lough Derg, opposite Portroe, which has a very ancient and illustrious history. It is small in area, not more than two score acres or less, but in the early days of the Church in Ireland it was the site of one of the great schools of Thomond. The island is called Iniscaltra, and the seat of learning of which it was the home was one of the greatest schools in Ireland during the seventh and eighth centuries. The school was founded by St Columba, of Terryglass. He died in 552. Another great man, and a more famous scholar than St Columba, ruled in Iniscaltra a hundred years later. His name was Caimin. Iniscaltra is deserted and silent now; and the tall round tower merely calls attention to the spot where once stood the church and schools. There is not a word of all this in the guide books. Nine out of every ten tourists who pass it on the Shannon pleasure steamers give it but a careless glance, and think no more about it. Only a round tower—another of them—and a few crumbling walls, and nothing more but green, green rich grass and Galway cattle. Yet there was a time when scholars came hither from many lands. A scion of the Lagenian race and the descendant of a Leinster king was its rector. He was the trusted friend of St Finian of Clonard, and one whose word went far in the councils of the sages and scholars of Erin.

The road turns southward, now running close to the waterside, through scenery which it would be hard to surpass in beauty even in Ireland. You have to loiter here and there and fill your eyes with pictures of the blue water and the green fields and the noble woods—all to be retained in the memory and carried away. There is scarcely a sound, only the soft voice of the wavelets on the shore, and the splash of a fish leaping after a fly, and the low song of the trees. But this soft harmony is ripped open by the grating hen-like note of a pheasant in a whin clump under the pines, and through the slit in the pulsating silence come far-off voices over the water, from a sail boat gliding leisurely down stream. I am encamped in a tangle of grass and bracken, with the tuneful woods above me and the Shannon spread out below, and I find it very fresh and sweet and restful. I climbed in here over a wall, swinging myself down from it by the branches of a tree. There was a notice board on the wall prohibiting people from 'trespassing', so I supposed I am on somebody's preserves, but the thought does not cause me any uneasiness. I am in possession for the moment, and that is enough. It is all mine for the time being. It is entirely splendid, and I am thinking of going to sleep when I hear a big rustling close at hand in the under-brush. I lean up on my elbow from my recumbent position, and parting the tangle around me with a gentle kick which fills the air with the healthy breath of torn fern stalks, I proceed to reconnoitre the intrusion. It is a man with a fish-ing rod and a basket, and he walks into the glade with the air of one whose proprietary rights in the soil are unquest-ionable before the law. He sees me, and a frown gathers upon his face as he comes towards me. He speaks to me in a language almost devoid of 'r's' and says, 'What awe you doing heawh?'

I catch my boot toes argumentatively, and regard him in cold reproof. But the only thing I can bring myself to say to him is:

'Are you accustomed to speak to people before you are introduced to them?'

'I am accustomed to deal legally with trespassaws, and will now thank you to take youawself out of this.'

'And who are you?'

'The ownagh.'

'The owner!' and I swept my hand out towards the

62

water and the distant mountains, and backward to indicate the singing in the trees. 'You own all this? You? No, *a chara*, you are mistaken. Try again.'

'Try again?' he fumed. 'I'll teach you who I am—'

'Oh! go away,' I said, wearily, turning from him. 'Your attitude of mind towards first principles needs overhauling. I have ridden over fifty miles today, and you fatigue me.'

I lay back amongst the ferns once more, and closed my eyes to indicate that I considered the interview ended. He stormed round the locality for a few minutes, speaking about law and police and prosecution, and other tiresome subjects. But I took no further notice of him, and he soon grew weary of his own conversation and left me. Then I went back to my wheel, over the wall, and resumed my journey.

A few more miles of the same beautiful scenery. Then a squeezing together of the hedgerows, and the roofs of a township, and the dark grey belfry of a church; a twelve-arch bridge; a few silvery miles of water; a long vista of square fields sloping westward to a wide wild sweep of mountain, and I was riding into ancient Killaloe.

Killaloe is becoming fashionable, and the tourist who fishes and plays golf, and drinks Scotch whiskey, is now an unlovely feature of the landscape. I believe someone belonging to the royal family of England passed up the Shannon a few years ago, and said that Killaloe was quite a picturesque place. Ever since the angling, golfing, whiskeying tourists have patronised the place. You see them trying to catch fish with the wrong fly, and 'catching crabs' with right or left oar as they try to row boats along the river. And you hear them at their golf talk as they greet each other at the railway station. But they can only do a little, a very little, to spoil Killaloe. It sees them go and come, and makes a little money out of them, and takes care that they pay cash for all value received. They cannot vulgarise the ancient renown of Kincora, or filch a laurel leaf from the wreath of King Brian, or dim the holy lustre that abides round the name of St Finnan.

Above the bridge, overlooking the river, are the ruins of Kincora. This was the palace of the kings of the Dalcassian race—the proud descendants of Heber, who won the sovereignty of Erin from the Hy-Niall, and raised Thomond from the position of a third or fourth-rate chieftainry until it became the hegemony of Ireland. It was to Kincora that a bedraggled horseman galloped with the bloody tidings that Mahon, King of Munster, had been treacherously murdered in the mountains of Knockinreorin, and when the tale was told in the halls of the Thomond palace, a prince, the brother of the murdered king, took down his harp from the wall, and, in a wild outburst of grief, chanted a song of lament and of revenge. This prince's name was Brian, afterwards to be known as Brian Boru, or Borumha—that is, Brian of the Tribute, High King of Ireland, lawgiver, statesman, warrior, and the deliverer of his country.

The death of Mahon is described in the *Wars of the Gaedhill and the Gall*, and is one of the saddest and most tragic events in the history of the race of Heber. He was an energetic, hard-hitting, wise kind of man, and had by his own right hand won the sovereignty of Munster. He drove the Danes out of Thomond, sailed his ships from Lough Derg to the sea, and was acknowledged as ruler by all the chieftains of Desmond. Like most men who fight their way to power, he had made many enemies, and amongst the most bitter of those who hated and envied him were the chieftains of the Eoghanacht. Donovan MacCathal, of Hy-Fidhgente, and Molloy, the Chieftain of Desmond, leagued with the Danish general to bring about the downfall of the head of the Dalcassians, and between them they swore that

64

Mahon shoud die. They invited him to a friendly conference at Donovan's house, in order to discuss certain affairs
of state. Mahon accepted the invitation, and set out to keep
the appointment. Some suspicion he must have had, or
some warning he must have received, for he placed himself
under the protection of the clergy, and took with him,
encased in a costly shrine, a copy of the Gospels, made by
the hand of St Finbar. This sacred treasure was taken from
Cork to Mahon specially for the occasion, and the Munster
king, once in possession of it, believed himself safe against
the machinations of open or secret foes. There seems to
have been some difference between Mahon and his tributary chieftains, and that the Bishop of Cork guaranteed that
each person assisting at the friendly conference should be
under episcopal protection. On his way thither, Mahon was
treacherously seized by Donovan, who, in accordance with
the agreement entered into with his confederates, sent the
royal prisoner to the Chieftain of Desmond. The Bishop of
Cork, and Molloy were waiting for Mahon at Sliabh Cacin,
on one of the slopes of the gorge or gap through which the
road passed. The Hy-Fidhgente men and their prisoner were
on the opposite slope, and on reaching the spot agreed
upon the murderers' steel leaped upon the air. When Mahon
saw that his captors were turning their swords against his
life, he threw the sacred scroll and the shrine to a priest
who accompanied him, so that the blood of a murdered
man might not stain it. In a few minutes he was a gory
corpse, and his assassins were wiping his heart's blood from
their swords. The Bishop of Cork saw the flashing of their
steel from his position beside the Desmond Chief on the
opposite hill, and hurried to the scene of blood.

'What can I do? Oh, tell me what am I to do?' he said,
appealing to Molloy.

'Go and cure the patient; you will find him lying yonder,'

was the answer given in savage irony.

When the horrified prelate reached the opposite slope of the gap good King Mahon was no more.

Some historians say that Mahon was not taking the sacred book with him for protection, but that he had caused it to be brought to him so that upon it his tributary chieftains might swear their fealty. Others say that when he was attacked he clutched the Gospels to his heart to shield him from the swords of his foes, and that the shrine and its contents were stained with his heart's blood. Mahon was buried where he fell, and it is said that over his grave the bishop 'wept bitterly, and uttered a prophecy concerning the future fate of the murderers' which was fulfilled with a swift and fierce exactness.

In no heart was such sorrow and rage caused by the murder of Mahon as in the heart of Brian. His song of lament has been given an interpretation in English by 'The Bard of Thomond', and has often been quoted. A verse or two may, without apology, be inserted here:

> Oh, Mahon, my brother, we've conquered
>   And marched side by side,
> And thou wert to the love of my soul
>   As a beautiful bride;
> In the battle, the banquet, the council,
>   The chase and the throne,
> Our beings were blended —our spirits
>   Were filled with one tone.
>
> Oh, Mahon, my brother, thou'st died
>   Like the hind of the wood,
> The hand of assassins were red
>   With thy pure, noble blood;
> And I was not near my beloved
>   When thou wast o'erpowered,
> To steep in their heart's blood the steel
>   Of my blue-beaming sword.

66

It galled Brian terribly that his brother had been slaughtered unarmed. Had Mahon died fighting against a hundred, Brian would have found some consolation in the proud thought that his brother had fallen like a king. Another fine verse is the following:

> Gold, silver, and jewels were only
> As dust in his hand,
> But his sword like a lightning-flash blasted
> The foes of the land.

Although his breast was torn with fraternal grief, Brian lost no time in punishing the criminals. He fell upon the Danes, slaying their leader, Ivar, and his son, and many of their followers. The chief of the Hy-Fidhgente was killed in battle, and for many years after his clan suffered for his crime. As for the Chieftain of Desmond, whose sword was the first to enter Mahon's breast, he was hunted like a wolf through the mountains for two years, and finally taken prisoner. He was put to death close to the spot where he had committed his infamous crime, and he was buried on the northern slopes of the pass, where the sun never shines upon his grave.

When Brian ascended the throne he was in his thirty-fifth year. Those who had followed him through a hundred fights against the Danes knew that he was a born soldier. But only one or two of the bards knew that in him Munster and Ireland would find the wise head and the fearless hand and the high and holy purpose of a great and kingly man. The utter defeat of the Danes at Clontarf cannot be thoroughly appreciated as a military achievement unless the student of history learns how Brian organised his victory. His long contest for supremacy with Malachy the Great was part of the work which he had set himself. He was greater than Malachy and he won, and won with honour and profit, for he enrolled his beaten opponent under his own banner, and was able to trust him as an ally. Brian saw that the Danes would rule in Ireland so long as Ireland was divided into petty kingdoms. He saw that the evil of provincialism would have to be trampled down if a true national ideal was to prosper, and he trampled down provincialism. It was not for Munster alone that Brian was ambitious, but for the whole of Ireland. Some of the more stubborn northerners held aloof from him, but otherwise it was practically a united nation that he hurled at the Danes on that Good Friday morning of the year 1014. If he had survived the battle, Ireland would have reaped the full harvest of his victory. As it was, he showed the way and the only way to every Irish leader who has drawn a sword or lifted a voice for Irish freedom ever since. That lesson is Unity—not the mere unity of the people who think alike, but the unity of the whole people in a national purpose, not mere unity of creed to combat creed, but the unity of men of every creed to combat the common enemy. No Ulster, Munster, Leinster, Connacht, or Meath, no North or South or East or West, no fatuous provincialism, no petty parochialism, but Ireland first and last and always.

That is one of the lessons which may be learned, or rehearsed, or repeated as you sit within the ruins of Kincora. There is another lesson, too, and a very important one. We must not expect that our great ones can be more than human. The man who will do most for Ireland is the man who says little about a thing until it is done. And he must know how to play the game as Brian played it. Ireland must learn to be patient with him—so long as he plays the game for her. An honest man who knows how to play the game, a man deeply and unchangeably Irish in his love and his hate, but a man who will not wear his heart on his sleeve, that is the man who will do mighty things.

I visited St Finnan's Cathedral, which is a good specimen of Norman ecclesiastical architecture. But St Finnan's Oratory is a building of quite a different kind. It is a standing proof of the high plane to which art was rapidly rising in Ireland, over a thousand years ago. The roof is of stone, and the arched doorway is well constructed. It is not so elaborate as the doorway of the Cathedral of Clonfert, nor so well preserved as the doorway of Devorgilla's Chapel at Clonmacnoise, but it is an excellent specimen of its kind and worthy of study. The Cathedral was erected by King Donald of Thomond before the coming of the Normans.

I tarried for half an hour on the bridge, and watched the shadows lengthen on the water, and on the sunny slopes over the town. The evening gold was deepening along the crests of the hills of Clare as I came within earshot of the rapids of Castleconnell. The Shannon is in a playful mood at this point, and for three or four hundred yards its course leaps and tumbles and breaks into cataracts, and churns itself into foam as white as the bark of the birch trees which look down upon the romping current. And as if the salmon were infected with the boisterous mood of the river, they put their tails in their mouths and leap from the foamy pools underneath the falls into the smooth water above. There is another salmon leap at Meelick, above Lough Derg, and even a better one than at Castleconnell. There is a certain fascination in watching the big fish take the leap and make it. Sometimes a fish will fail once or twice. But another and stronger effort whirls it like a huge half moon of golden green through the sunshine over the point where the glassy current breaks into a foamy torrent, and throws itself roaring down the fall. It is told in the old Irish legends that long ago, there were men upon the world who could leap like a salmon. Cuchulain was one of them. On his great fight at the Ford of the Boyne this 'hero leap' of his came frequently into play, and it was one of the means by which he could baffle and defeat his foes.

The red sun was sinking behind the mountains as I took to the wheel again. A few more miles now in the rosy afterglow, a hill or two, a long shaded downward gradient, then a spin along the level. I was on the sidewalk now running smoothly, and wondering if I would reach my journey's end before dark. I did it. A turn in the road brought me within view of the suburbs, and in the dew-laden gloaming I rode into Limerick. The cyclometer registered seventy miles, and I would not sell the tamest of them for a free pass on a railway.

5

Limerick the Heroic – The City that takes Life as it comes –
Industrial Limerick – A Queerly Placed Monument on Sars-
field Bridge – The Siege – Sarsfield's Raid to Ballyneety –
The Old Walls – 'The Black Gate' – Sarsfield's Fatal Ingen-
uousness – The O'Connell Monument – George's Street –
St John's – St Mary's – The Founder of Limerick – The
Limerick Dogs – Garryowen and 'Johnny Collins' – Gerald
Griffin – Lord Dunraven and the Game of Poker.

After a hungry cyclist's supper at one of the hotels and
Limerick has some good hotels—I strolled through the city
by lamplight. Next morning I was astir early and had made
a tour of the principal streets before breakfast. I made
several other tours during the day, and found much that
was interesting at every other turn and crossing. It would
have been the same if I had stayed for a week. Limerick is
packed with great memories. It breathes history. Even its
very stone-heaps are eloquent. I crossed the river over and
over again, strolled through Garryowen, and through the
streets where the great Munster fair is held, out to the reservoir. I prowled around the old parts of the city and
through the more modern streets, visited all that is left of
the walls, saw where the fighting was hottest, sat on the
river, rested beside the Treaty Stone, lounged on the
bridges, stood at shop doors and at street corners looking at
the faces of the passers-by, and when the time came for me
to leave I was sorry. I arrived there prejudiced in its favour.
Consequently I liked it to some extent before I saw it. I
liked the imperfect view I got of it as I entered it in the

71

gloaming. I liked it ten times better when I saw it in the light of day. I liked it better than ever when I was leaving it, not because I was parting from it, for I have told you I was sorry to go, but just because it had grown upon me.

And yet, as far as appearances go, Limerick is not a show place. It is a quiet old town a good deal dilapidated here and there, not by any means tidy or methodical, nor by any means over-clean, even in the most central streets, grim and grimy and sombre-looking, but very lovable. I saw a youth of nineteen or twenty summers working mightily on the quays discharging cargo from a steamer. He was poorly clad; shirt and pants were quilted with patches; yet vigour was in his cheeks and laughter in his eyes; and he seemed ready for the worst that fortune might send him. He struck me as being, in a certain sense, the incarnation of the spirit of his native city. For Limerick, too, works hard, is careless of appearance, is apparently devil-may-care in many things, and defiant of fate. Its defiance is not strident or theatrical. There is nothing blatant or melodramatic about Limerick at all. It seems to regard destiny with genial mockery, flinging a challenge from out its battered walls amidst a peal of musical laughter.

When you analyse your impressions of places you have seen, you often find them associated with some particular colour—white or brown, or black, or skyblue, or yellow or red. Grey is the colour that rises before me when I think of Limerick—dark grey, steel grey, pearl grey, bluish grey. Its walls and roofs and streets are grey. The morning sky over it was grey. The wide river was thinly veiled with greyish mist. There were grey hazes on the Thomond fields and in the southern distances. But this greyness is not the fading of age. I cannot think of Limerick as being stricken in years. You meet occasionally a man in the world who is independent of circumstances, who is superior to every depressing

72

and deprecating prank of adversity, who is independent in thought, untamed in soul, in spite of everything, who is out-at-elbows but unashamed—a weather-beaten, healthy, lovable heroic kind of tatterdemalion. Well, as with men, so with cities. Each has an individuality. The individuality of Limerick is that of the man I have described. At least that is my impression of it. Another man may go thither and find it a dudish, perfumed, fastidious, starched, and hot-ironed individuality. I did not.

There is a good deal of industrial enterprise in Limerick, although, of course, there is room for a good deal more. There is a flour-milling industry. The wheat is foreign but the millers are Irish, and so, I was told, is the market for the output. There is a thriving bacon-curing industry also carried on, which gives constant employment to numerous hands. I know also that there is a tannery. I saw the signboard over a door, and there were unmistakable odours on the air. I was told that long ago the Limerick leather trade was more important than at present. I was sorry to hear this, although, doubtless, a tannery is not a very fragrant next-door neighbour to have. I met large automobile vans in the suburbs, laden heavily with big cream cans, coming in from the country dairies. There is a big butter-making industry in the city, and it ought to be prosperous considering the constant supplies which it is able to procure under favourable conditions. There was a great lace-making industry long ago in Limerick. It went down in the disastrous industrial decline of Ireland under the Union. But the art of making the beautiful Limerick lace has not been lost, and I noticed a lace school during my rambles. May it succeed. May everything succeed that is honestly trying to create employment in Ireland, thus enabling many to make a decent living in their own country who have now to cross the sea to earn a living wage amongst strangers.

The shipping interests of Limerick are far from being what they once were. They are nothing like what they would be if Ireland were governed in the interests of the people of Ireland. When you see the splendid estuary, the wide stream, the spacious quays, the rich country beyond the city, and then look at a steamer or two, and half-a-dozen schooners, and a few lighters where there should be scores of sea-going vessels, you realise that Ireland is a captive nation, and that her captors robbed her of trade as well as of everything else but her faith and honour.

When I stood on Sarsfield Bridge first, it was on the night of my arrival. There was but a faint light from the gas lamps, but the partial darkness did not hide a statue which stands behind the eastern battlement with a cannon on each side of the pedestal.

'It will be the Sarsfield monument,' I said in my own mind, and resolved that I would revisit it early next morning. The daylight revealed to me the curious fact that this statue on Sarsfield Bridge was not erected to Sarsfield or to any other Irish patriot, but to some huzzar officer of the English army who took part in the charge of Balaclava. It seemed wonderful just at first. The monument itself did not impress me greatly as a work of art. Like a fly in amber,

> It was not that the thing was rich or rare,
> You wondered how the devil it got there.

However, when your second thoughts began to work, the location of such a monument in such a place was soon explained. It was there for the same reaons that the monument to Dutch William stands before the old Parliament House in College Green, Dublin, for the same reasons that a monument to Nelson stands in O'Connell Street, Dublin. It is all part of the scheme to Anglicise the Irish mind, to glorify things English in Ireland, to make English heroes the heroes of the Irish people, to accustom the Irish patriot to the constant presence in his native land of the rule and might and meanness of the Saxon. This monument on Sarsfield Bridge was erected to the memory of one Viscount Fitzgibbon, who was probably some local landlord. In any case he was certainly a man who never drew a sword for Ireland, and never was loyal to her. The face, as portrayed by the sculptor, is rather a weak one. But the brazen lips give and insolent message to Limerick all the same, which may be interpreted as follows:

'You called this bridge after a man who won glory for Limerick and for Ireland, but I am here to remind you of a man who drew the sword for your masters. You celebrate the military and civic fame of your city in the name you give this bridge, but I am here to remind you that neither the valour nor the genius of your sires sufficed to prevail against England. The name of this bridge stands for Ireland; I stand for England. I am here to glorify enlistment. I am a tout for the recruiting-sergeant. I am here because ye are partially tamed. I tell ye to be tamer still. Be peaceful through and through, and thank God ye are slaves. Come to heel, ye helots. Croppies lie down!'

I found the Sarsfield monument next morning after considerable search. It stands beyond the Catholic Cathedral of St John in the cathedral grounds upon a site granted to the trustees by the Right Rev. George Butler, Lord Bishop of Limerick. It is not inappropriately located, for it cannot be far from the place where the fighting on the wall was hottest. The monument itself can lay very little claim to be a triumph of art. It is not worthy of Sarsfield at all. But then the hero of Ballyneety needs no bronze or marble to perpetuate his fame. There is a park in Limerick ornamented by a lofty monument to some local magnate who represented the constituency once in the British Parliament. The

75

pedestal upon which his statue is placed is many times higher than the Sarsfield monument. But the fame of the Irish general will flourish centuries after the name of the magnate shall have been forgotten.

I crossed the Thomond Bridge to the Clare side of the river, and located as well as I could the encampment of Sarsfield's cavalry on that memorable Sunday evening in the August of 1690. I laid my bicycle against a wall, and leaning against the doorway of a roofless cabin, I called back the past into the present. It is one of the privileges of rambling. There are 38,000 English, Dutch and Anglo-Irish besiegers on the southern bank of the river, and they are confident of a speedy victory. Dutch William himself arrived from Cahirconlish yesterday and spent the day marking out positions for his siege artillery. There is a leaden war cloud over Limerick, and it appears to be only a question of hours when the storm will burst upon the beleagured city and sweep its resistance away. There are scarcely 10,000 men to guard the defences, and a great part of the war stores, arms and ammunition have been carted off to Galway by those carpet soldiers—Tyrconnel and Lauzun—who left the Irish lines confident that the walls could be battered down 'with roasted apples'. But Sarsfield and Berwick and De Boisseleau have decided to remain and defend the city, and the citizens—to their undying glory—have decided to stand by them, come what may. Even now they are out in their numbers, men and women of every rank and age, with their children, helping De Boisseleau's engineers to strengthen the defences. But there is a siege train coming to the English from Waterford, with guns strong enough to lay the city in ruins, and, worse than all, there is a pontoon bridge coming which, if placed in position, will allow William's forces to cross the Shannon and take the city in the rear. Guns, caissons, bridges, and stores are all together in the hills to the southward marching steadily to join the besiegers.

It is of this that Sarsfield has been thinking all day and all yesterday, consulting with De Boisseleau, consulting with a few of his officers, consulting also with a certain Rapparee leader who has ridden in from the mountains, keeping his thoughts to himself mostly, this noble Sarsfield, but planning and preparing one of the most effective and splendid cavalry raids recorded in history. He has given certain orders now, and five hundred chosen riders are standing, bridle in hand, awaiting the word to mount. It is dark and late when the Chief swings himself on horseback and sends his commands quietly down the line. There is no bugle call, no roll of drum, no hoarsely shouted order flung from mouth to mouth by the squadron leaders. A half-whispered phrase in Irish—for Sarsfield and his troopers are Irish speakers—a low thunder of hoofs, and then, as silently as may be, they take themselves off into the darkness. They ford the Shannon at Ballvelly, and the dawn of Monday morning finds them on the march through Tipperary. Beside the general rides a guide whose fame is to go down to posterity. He is the daring Rapparee horseman, known as 'Galloping O'Hogan', who has the secret of every ravine in the Silvermines and every glen of the Keepers, who knows every ford and togher and boreen by heart, and who will conduct the Irish horsemen into the midst of the English convoy before a hoof-stroke is heard and before a blow is struck. Silently as possible out of the mountain passes, where a halt had been made to reconnoitre, silently as possible over the plains, quietly, steadily, surely, by wood and stream and hill, through the soft darkness, the dauntless cavalcade is riding into history. The watchword of the English was learned hours ago as the darkness fell. By a strange coincidence it is 'Sarsfield'. At three o'clock on Tuesday morning the great deed is done. The drowsy

English sentry challenges and demands the countersign from the horsemen advancing over the picket line. It comes in a ringing voice, and accompanied by a sabre cut: 'Sarsfield is the word and Sarsfield is the man.' Five hundred chargers leap in amongst the sleepers, and five hundred thirsty sabres are at work amongst the panic-stricken soldiery who come hurrying from their tents. Through the camp and back again and once more from end to end sweep the riders of Limerick; and that is enough. The gunners are cut down, or flying, and the siege-train is at Sarsfield's mercy. He has the guns filled with powder and their snouts buried in the ground. The pontoons are heaped upon the overturned carriages and caissons, a train is fired, and the earth and sky for miles around are reddened with the flash with which the mass goes upward in scrap iron. The thunder of the explosion bellowed into the English trenches before Limerick and brought William from his slumbers. Too late. The sentry reports that just now the sky was ablaze like the noonday; and William knows that the big guns and bridges, and his tons of powder and ball have been scooped up and destroyed. Five hundred men were despatched from William's camp last night to join the convoy; for some rumour that Sarsfield was abroad had been brought in. Two more bodies of horse are now sent forth to cut off the Irish cavalry on its return gallop. But the Rapparees are scouting along the hills, and O'Hogan himself is still with the squadrons of the victors. There are joyous cheers along the Shannon when evening comes, for all Limerick is out to welcome the heroes. The Irish guns beyond the river fronting the English batteries give tongue in a salute, and the very echo in the staunch old city is roused by the cannonade and the cheering as the troopers from Ballyneety come trotting in.

It was a glorious raid. What would you not have given to

take part it it!

I went to St John's Hospital and saw some of the old walls. There are a tower and gateway there which still show marks of the bombardment. There is a stone trough too, and they call it after Sarsfield. The tower is part of the hospital, and the wall near it serves as part of one of the hospital buildings. Just outside the hospital grounds is another gate. They call it the 'Black Battery' and also the 'Black Gate'. There was terrible fighting about here. On 27 August ten thousand men were hurled by William at a breach which his cannon had made in the walls. The first onset was partially succcessful. Battalion after battalion was sent into the breach and the defence was broken down. The assailants poured into the city cheering for victory. But it was only then that their fight was beginning, although they looked upon it as ended. From every street and lane and bridge and passage came men and women, armed with whatever weapons they could find. They faced the cheering enemy and a terrible street fight began. The blacksmith struck home with his sledge, the butcher with his cleaver, the labourer with his spade, the children threw stones from the windows, the women, armed with broken bottles and knives and staves, fought like furies through the English, down the streets, into the very breach, where they died beside the men. A few squadrons of Sarsfield's horsemen galloped across the bridges from the Clare side of the river and joined the fray. Blood ran like water, and splashed red in the gutters. The streets were turned into shambles, but the fight went on and on. The English were forced to give way. Foot by foot they were pressed back to the breach and then through it, home to their entrenchments. The Irish pursued them into their very camp; but instead of continuing the slaughter of the routed foe they helped to extinguish the flames which threatened to consume the Williamite hospital. Some of the Irish even helped to remove the wounded from the burning building! Meanwhile the Brandenburghers have effected a kind of flank movement and are swarming over a battery near the breach. But the mine is ready for them and is fired at the right moment. The earth under the battery opens as if hell were bursting through from below, and in a sickening, hollow, deafening roar the ground is ripped to pieces and the storming regiment is hurled skyward, a mass of mangled corpses. Irish and English stand as if spellbound for some seconds, and then an Irish cheer of triumph rings out along the walls. William cannot induce his soldiers to return to the assault next day, and in disgust goes back to England. The besieging army struck camp during the night and left Limerick in peace.

The victory so splendidly won was unfortunately barren in results. It was the fault of James and of his courtier creatures, Tyrconnel and Lauzun. Had the Galway garrison been ordered to stay, had the truth of the Irish situation been laid before Louis by James, the contemptible runaway from the Boyne, had the fight been for Irish freedom instead of for one of the worthless and faithless Stuarts, had Sarsfield been a negotiator as well as a soldier, then the history of Ireland would have had a different trend, God knows, through the centuries that have come and gone since the accursed Treaty of Limerick was made and broken.

Sarsfield was a soldier, but he was not a diplomat. He was fitted to an Irish general, although he bore an English-made title, and although he had borne arms for England and had fought her battles. His heart was Irish, and his last words on the field of Landen, far away from Ireland, proved that he loved her well. But the man Ireland wanted then was a Sarsfield who could play the game. One hour of such a man after Limerick would have been worth a hundred of men taking clots of their hearts' blood in their hands on foreign battlefields, to say how much they wished it had been shed for Ireland. All honour to the brave and chivalrous soldier who defended Limerick. But, oh! if he had been another Shane the Proud! A Shane would have led a man like St Ruth by the nose, or mopped his tent-floor with him. He would also have conducted the negotiations after the siege of 1691 so that there would have been a loophole left open by which advantage could have been taken of the altered circumstances brought about by the arrival of the French auxiliary expedition with money, arms, and provisions.

The Treaty Stone is at the Clare end of Thomond Bridge. It stands on a granite pedestal now, for the souvenir-hunters were gradually chipping it away. When the Treaty was signed on it, however, it lay on the ground on the river bank, and around it, on the morning of 3 October, Sarsfield and his lieutenants met De Ginkell and the Lords Justices, and signed the solemn covenant which was broken ''ere the ink wherewith 'twas writ could dry'.

Two days afterwards the Irish army marched out and signified its choice to cross the seas and fight under the flag of France. Within a week the French relieving expedition arrived. But there was no proviso in the Treaty for such a contingency. Sarsfield said that even if a hundred thousand Frenchmen offered to fight for Ireland now there was nothing for it but to say that the fight could not be— because the Treaty was signed. He would keep faith with England. So would Shane, but Shane would have held out for guarantees. Shane would have negotiated like a man who knew how to play the game. Of course England never for a moment meant to keep faith with Sarsfield. If Sarsfield had been a Shane O'Neill he would have looked upon this as axiomatic, and would have kept it steadily in view.

As it was, he did not take it into account at all—for, alas! he was only a lion-hearted, splendid, chivalrous soldier, and knew nothing about the art of playing the game.

When the Treaty was broken—shamelessly and infamously broken—and when Ireland from end to end groaned, generation after generation, under the Penal Laws, it was only a very poor consolation to the down-trodden people to know that Irish valour was winning victories for other peoples, and that Irish genius was adorning the statesmanship of other nations.

Glory of the Irelands beyond the seas! Glory of the Irish in exile! Glory of the Irish race! Glory of the racial ideal! Of what good is it all to Ireland? The battle for Ireland must be fought in Ireland, by the people of Ireland. Every strong arm and every true heart that leaves Ireland is more or less a loss to Ireland, and this was as true after Limerick as it is today.

There is a monument to O'Connell in George's Street, by Hogan. The statue is very gracefully draped, but the treatment of the cloak is not very fortunate. The folds are twisted round the lower part of the figure, hampering the legs and feet. If the statue were draped as a Roman tribune or as as Grecian philosopher, this arrangement of the cloak might not be out of place, but in the broadcloth costume of the early nineteenth century it seems theatrical, exaggerated, and lacking in manly dignity. Foley's manipulation of the cloak is more adequate and convincing. As a matter of fact the monument over O'Connell Bridge is one of the great masterpieces of modern statuary, and does much to redeem the awful decadence of art that fell upon Ireland as one of the curses of her oppression.

I do not know what particular George gave his name to the principal street in Limerick. Probably it was one of the Georges who sat on the throne of England, and who hated

Ireland. It is a very fine street, this George's Street, and is unspoiled by tramlines. Limerick has yet to adopt the tramcar. Up to the present it has got along very well without it. Most of the big shops are on George's Street, but there are other important business streets. The industrial establishments are along the water front or in the outskirts of the city. The railway station is conveniently situated, being only a few minutes' walk from George's Street.

Speaking about the Georges of Hanover and England recalls another English sovereign in connection with Limerick. King John visited Limerick once upon a time—in the year 1210, to be more exact. He ordered a big castle to be built there, partly to commemorate his visit, and partly to overawe the Thomond people. The castle is still there on the southern bank of the river, looming over Thomond Bridge. It is the most perfect type of Norman military architecture in Ireland. It is in good repair, and is used as a barrack. King John was the only English monarch that ever visited Limerick, and for this small mercy Limerick is duly thankful. William of Orange was in the neighbourhood for a while, as we have seen, trying to gain an entrance into Limerick society, but he was disappointed.

The Catholic Cathedral of St John's is a beautiful edifice. It is well situated, and its slender spire, which is 280 feet high, can be seen from many parts of the city and within a radius of several miles. The style is Gothic, but not of the flamboyant school, and very chaste and graceful in design. I confess to a feeling of relief whenever I meet a modern Irish church that departs from the stereo-typed Gothic style. I was glad to hear of a church of the Irish style of architecture having been commenced at Spiddal, Galway, not long ago, because I regarded it as straw on the ever-swelling current of Irish thought, as distinguished from English and foreign thought, which has so long held sway in Ireland.

When I think of the ruined churches along the Shannon I know that we were on the road to create or evolve a distintive school of architecture of our own when the calamities of the twelfth century fell upon us. This school would not have been Gothic nor Norman nor Romanesque nor Greek. It would have been Irish. It would not have been an original school. Neither is the Gothic. Neither is the Greek. Perhaps the only original things in any architecture are the elemental things, the things suggested by the tent pole, the ridge pole, the doorway and whatever served as a roof. The Irish school of architecture would have been distinctive, in as much as it would have reflected the artistic temperament of our forefathers. We know by the relics of art that have come down to us from them that they had a keen sense of beauty. Their achievements in design, so far as they went, were marvellous. Their spirals and interlacings and treatment of colour have won admiration from all impartial critics of modern times. It is certain that they would have developed a wider sense of proportion and arrived at a truer estimate of values. Modern Ireland has done some very fine Gothic work, but the finer the work the more perfect is the imitation, and that is all that can be said for it. Imitation is not always good and is often bad. Gothic is very beautiful, but it would do Ireland no harm if she had less of it and more of her own. Anything, whether in art or industry or letters, that tends to make a nation self-centred is good. Once she is self-centred it is no harm for her to dabble in a little imitation. But self-reliance is never fostered by leaning on other people. The development of native art is an essential part of nation-building, and few arts can be made to have a more noble influence upon taste than a native school of architecture.

St Mary's was the old Catholic Cathedral of Limerick. It was wrested from the Catholics during the great sequestrations, confiscations, annexations, plantations, conciliations, undertakings, or whatever name you choose to give to the big steals and highway robberies that the English perpetrated in Ireland. I think it was the same King Donald who built the Cathedral of St Finnan at Killaloe, that donated St Mary's to Limerick. His right name was Domnal Mor. He was the last King of Cashel. He was the great-grandson of Tordelbach, King of Ireland, the first man who ever bore the name of O'Brien. Tordelbach O'Brien was the son of Tadg, who was the son of King Brian Borumha. When Tordelbach called himself Ua-Briain (O'Brien), he meant to have it known that he was the grandson of the hero of Clontarf. Like his great and pious ancestor, the last King of Cashel was a church-builder on a kingly scale. Part of his tomb is still in the Cathedral. Doubtless the whole of it would be there only for the Cromwellian cavalry. Those puritanical vandals stabled their horses in the sacred edifice while they were in Limerick and greatly defaced the tombs and other monuments with which the place was adorned. There is some fine woodcarving in the choir and nave, and the ruined cloister facing the street shows upon what an elaborate scale the building was originally designed.

It was St Munchin who founded the first church in Limerick late in the sixth or early in the seventh century. He was named Muchin the Wise, and was of the Dalcassian race, being directly descended from the great Cormac Cas himself. He ruled in Mungret Abbey for many years, and then in his old age retired and built himself an oratory and cell which the people call Cill-Munchin, or the Church of Munchin. It was the beginning of Limerick. The city grew around the cell of the aged saint, as Cork grew around the oratory of St Finnbar.

I strolled along the southern fringe of the city farthest from the river, struck out from a remnant of the old wall in Clare Street, and headed westward through a labyrinthine jungle of back lanes, alleys, and roofless houses. It appeared to be rather an exclusive quarter in a certain sense, and I doubted, after I have enmeshed myself in its sinuosities, that the general public patronised it very extensively as a place of recreation, or exercised the right of way through it, if such a right existed. It was a bow-legged dog with a fighting face that fixed this latter conclusion upon me by coming forward with all his hair standing and fire in his eyes, barking furiously. He was quickly joined by other dogs of excessive lung power. They stripped their teeth at me and advanced inch by inch, whether on a bluff or on real business, I could not say. To retreat would have been madness. To advance unarmed would have been imprudent. To remain inactive would have been to invite disaster. I therefore, in all modesty, and on a very small scale, engaged in diplomacy. In other words, I instigated and fomented a dog fight. I said: 'Catch him, Spot'; 'Bite him, Terry'; 'Beat him, Lad'; 'Choke him, William the Third, or whatever your name is' (he was a hook-nosed, select-looking, taciturn kind of dog that did most of his vituperation inwardly, as it were). I addressed the meeting in this strain for a few seconds, after which the battle began with great pomp and circumstance. One after another the dogs went out of commission, howling with pain, until only two champions were left—Lad and William the Third. I left them, hoping that William would get the worst of it. I came upon a few inhabited houses in an alley farther on and asked what part of the city I was in. A woman leant over a half-door and told me kindly that it was called 'English Town'. No doubt it was part of the camp or works that had been occupied by the English. I pursued my way uphill and made short cuts over wastes of stone heaps. It was the loneliest ramble I have ever taken in any city. I have prowled in the back streets of La Rochelle, Lisbon, Funchal, Santa Cruz de Teneriffe, Pernambuco, and Rio, but never felt so lonely as in 'English Town' in Limerick. It was not that I feared for my personal safety, but chiefly because there was no one to menace it. I questioned a few people I met regarding certain ruins which appeared to have been at one time somewhat pretentious buildings. One was an old jail, another the house of a former mayor, another a mansion once inhabited by a local shipowner, and so on. They were all roofless, weedgrown and windowless. Empty fire places and cut stone lintels stared out upon the grey desolation around them as if they were left to emphasise the extent of the ruin which had been wrought. Most of the roofless gables were of smaller houses. There seemed to be whole streets of battered-down cottages. Apparently it was a residential quarter of the working classes in former years. It is the home of bats, cats, and dogs now.

My next inquiry regarding my whereabouts brought out the information that I stood in Garryowen. I was west of St John's Cathedral now, and on sloping ground I caught sight of a piece of green sward farther away where some boys were playing. They were doing what is known as a tailor's tumble, a feat performed by holding your toes and going head over heels down hill like a wheel. They stood up at my approach, and replied to my good-morrow cheerily.

'Where is Johnny Collins?' I asked them.

They looked at each other, then at me, and then one of them answered:

'He isn't here!'

'What Johnny Collins do you mean?' I asked.

'I don't know,' was the answer.

'Do you know any Johnny Collins, any of you?'

They shook their heads.

'Never heard of any Johnny Collins? Come, now, think.'

They thought for a while, and then one of them brightened up and said:

'Oh, I know now. It's the man in the song.'

'How does the song go, do you remember?'

And he quoted instantly the lines referred to from *Garryowen*:

> There's Johnny Collins tall and straight,
>   He'd throw a bar of any weight
> From Garryowen to Thomond Gate
>   For Garryowen and glory.

He tapped his foot on the ground to the beat of the metre, and was doubtless thinking of the tune.

'Correct,' I said, as he finished. 'And now, can any of you give me another verse? If you can it means gingerbread and apples—'

'I can,' they all cried in chorus, interrupting me.

'Good,' I said. 'Then this young man with the yellow hair will give me a verse.' And he did.

> Though Garryowen has gone to wrack,
>   We'll win her olden glories back.
> The night, long, starless, cold and black,
>   We'll light with song and story.

We adjourned to a place of their choice where the distribution of prizes took place. Crowning the slope above the field in which I met them was a green mound like a modern fort. They told me it was the reservoir. It used to be the execution ground, and the old gibbet or flogging triangle is there yet.

Gerald Griffin was a Limerickman, and there is a street called after him. I mentioned his name casually to several people. They had all heard about him, but only a few had read him or knew of his work in Anglo-Irish literature. He does not appear to have ever impressed the popular mind.

His novels are scarcely read at all now. As for his poetry, outside of a few pieces, little of it is known. He lacked the deep intuition and the passionate love of country which breathe in Kickham's work, and which have made his name a household word in Tipperary.

I chartered a jaunting-car and drove round the city, holding desultory fragments of conversation with the driver, who was so well known in every district that half his time was occupied saying things to his friends. I asked him if there were any special place of interest within convenient reach of the city, and he offered to drive me to Adare on the most reasonable terms. Pretending ignorance, I asked him what was Adare.

'It's the place the poem was made about,' he explained, cracking his whip. 'Gerald Griffin, the man that one of the streets here is called after, wrote a poem about "Sweet Adare", sir, as he called it, and it's a grand place. Lord Dunraven, the man that made the Land Bill, lives there, sir. They call his place Adare Manor. Will we go out to it?'

'I have no time today. But tell me what kind of a man is Lord Dunraven?'

'Bedad, I don't know much about him, sir, except to see him now and then. He's a thin, spare, long-nosed, sharp-lookin' man. And they say he's fit to mind turkeys at a cross roads. I heard them talkin' about him th' other night in a bar down town, and one fellow a commercial traveller it was—said that Lord Dunraven was one of the cutest men in Ireland, and that he got the soft side of the Members of Parliament about the Land Bill. A very smart man, sir.'

'I'll tell you what an American gentleman said to me a few weeks ago, sir, as I was driving him back from Adare.'

'Had he spoken with Lord Dunraven?'

'No, sir, but I was telling him about the lord, and I think he had been readin' about him in the papers.'

'And what did he say?'

'"Well," says he, "this Lord Dunraven ought to be a great poker player." Do you know what kind of a game that is, sir?'

'I do,' I said. 'It is the game of life in a sense, and, to borrow your own words, my friend, the man who can mind turkeys at a cross road would be just the man to play a good hand at poker. Will you pull up, please, or do you mean to drive me into the water?'

He was laughing so heartily that he took no notice of his horse, although the animal was making a swaying kind of progress along the quay which brought the car alarmingly close to the brink of the river.

I paid him his fare, and then prepared to start. In another hour I was beating to the north-eastward facing homeward through the Golden Vale.

*　*　*　*　*

90

IN CONNEMARA
John M. Synge

Our breathless interest is sustained throughout this fascinating book as J. M. Synge shows us that 'one has to go a little way only to reach places and people that are typical of Connemara.' He paints a very moving picture of the reality of rural life in the west of Ireland. He admires the simplicity of the people's character, their skill in many varied crafts and their readiness to face risks and danger without any show of bravado. We hear the call of the wild and our professors are the fishermen, mountainy men and the people of the bogs. Synge's sympathy and delight with whatever was traditional enriches every page of this book.

As we visit Spiddal, Carraroe, Ballina, Belmullet and the inner lands of Mayo we frequently hear beautiful and striking phrases as we meet the fiery and magnificent peasants in their cottages.

IN WEST KERRY
John M. Synge

The most exciting way to learn about West Kerry is to see it through the eyes of one of Ireland's greatest dramatists, J. M. Synge, and let it weave its magic spell over us. He shows us the splendour of Kerry as we visit Dingle, Smerick Harbour, Sybil Ferriter's Castle, the Great Blasket, Tralee and we spend some time at the greatest event in Kerry — Puck Fair.

Synge invites us into the huts and cottages of the essentially Irish characters who had a dignity and settle peace that he not only noted but envied. According to Daniel Corkery, Synge preferred the happy-go-lucky folks who were not authorities on anything and their rambling stories that had not a word of truth in them to the pronouncements of the wise. Their companionship brings an unwonted delight and we relish the warmth of their hearts, their bright eyes, their reckless and astonounding talk as they lead us far away from the stifling streets of the cities and towns. We joyfully go with them over the hillsides, into the mountainy glens and across the bogs.

It is a little star-dust caught; a segment of the rainbow which I have clutched.

THE WIND THAT ROUND THE FASTNET SWEEPS

John M. Feehan

There are moments in the life of every human being when he becomes haunted with the longing to leave behind the turmoil and tension of daily living, to get away from it all and to escape to a clime where true peace can be found. There are many practical reasons why most of us cannot do this so the next best thing is to read the story of one who tried.

John M. Feehan sailed, all by himself, in a small boat around the coast of West Cork in a search for this Land of the Heart's Desire, this Isle of the Blest.

The result is a book which is not only a penetrating spiritual odyssey, but also a magnificent account of the wild rugged coastline, the peaceful harbours, and the strange unique characters he met in this unspoiled corner of Ireland. He writes with great charm, skill, sympathy and a mischievous roguish humour often at his own expense His sharp eye misses nothing. He sees the mystery, the beauty and the sense of wonder in ordinary things, and brings each situation to life so that the reader feels almost physically present during every moment of the cruise.

There is something for everyone in this book which is sure to bring joy and happiness to readers of all ages. It is a book that can be read again and again.

'... brilliant... the Irish Story of San Michele.' —

John B. Keane

THE MAGIC OF THE KERRY COAST
John M. Feehan

This is a sequel to the best selling *The Wind That Round the Fastnet Sweeps.* In it John M. Feehan continues his odyssey from Crookhaven up the coast of Kerry to the Skelling Rocks and the Blasket Islands, It follows the same pattern—a little sailing, a little thinking, a little laughing, a little drinking and once again we meet a marvellous collection of those strange and unusual characters who always seem to run across the author's path and which he describes with such understanding and humanity.

LETTERS FROM THE GREAT BLASKET
Eibhlis Ni Shulleabhain

This selection of *Letters from the Great Blasket*, for the most part written by Eibhlis Ni Shuilleabhain of the island to George Chambers in London, covers a period of over twenty years. Eibhlis married Sean O Criomhthain a son of Tomas O Criomhthain, *An tOileanach (The Islandman)*. On her marriage she lived in the same house as the Islandman and nursed him during the last years of his life which are described in the letters. Incidentally, the collection includes what must be an unique specimen of the Islandman's writing in English in the form of a letter expressing his goodwill towards Chambers.

Beginning in 1931 when the island was still a place where one might marry and raise a family (if only for certain exile in America) the letters end in 1951 with the author herself in exile on the mainland and 'the old folk of the island scattering to their graves.' By the time Eibhlis left the Blasket in July 1942 the island school had already closed and the three remaining pupils 'left to run wild with the rabbits.'

It must be remembered when reading these letters that they were written in a language foreign to Eibhlis whose native language was Irish. Only very minor changes were thought desirable in the letters and these in the interests of intelligibility. Here through the struggling idiom and laboured passages, emerges in fascinating detail a strange and different way of life as seen unconsciously through the eyes of a woman. This is not the island of the summer visitor but one intimately known, loved and feared—and finally abandoned.

THE MAN FROM CAPE CLEAR
Conchúr Ó Siocháin

Conchúr Ó Siocháin lived all his days on Cape Clear, the southern outpost of an old and deep-rooted civilisation. He lived as a farmer and a fisherman and his story vividly portrays life on that island which has Fastnet Rock as its nearest neighbour. He was a gifted storyteller, a craftsman and a discerning folklorist. Here he tells of life on the island drawing on the ancient traditions and the tales handed down from the dim past. There is a sense of humour, precision and a great sense of community on every page.

* * * * *

The Man from Cape Clear is a collection of memories and musings, topography and tales, and contains a fund of seafaring yarns not to be found elsewhere. It discloses aspects of insular life which should delight the inner eye of the world at large and enrich every Irishman's grasp of his heritage.